Formed of Fire

SELECTIONS IN CONTEMPORARY LAMPWORKED GLASS

FORMED OF FIRE
Selections in Contemporary Lampworked Glass
Bandhu S. Dunham

Salusa Glassworks, Incorporated
Prescott, Arizona, USA

Library of Congress Control Number: 2002093641

Dunham, Bandhu Scott, 1959-
   Formed of Fire
Contemporary Selections of Lampworked Glass / by Bandhu Scott Dunham
     128 p. 22.3 cm.
   ISBN 0-9658972-2-2
   1. Glass, blown, lampworked 2. Title.

Published by Salusa Glassworks, Inc.
P.O. Box 2354, Prescott, AZ 86302

Cover Illustration: Ginny Ruffner, *Smelling Surprise Flower Basket*,
10 inches high 22 inches wide 15 inches deep. Lampworked
borosilicate glass, sandblasted, mixed media. *Photo: Mike Seidl.*

Book Design: Kim Johansen, Black Dog Design • www.blackdogco.com

Printed in China

Formed of Fire

TABLE OF CONTENTS

KURT WALLSTAB

Vase, 21 cm high 5.6 cm diameter.
Lampworked soda lime glass; montage technique. *Photo: Courtesy of the Artist.*

Kurt Wallstab of Griesheim, Germany, is one
of the consummate masters of the montage
technique, which involves splicing individual
sections of colored tubing in complex patterns. The use of soda lime glass, which has
the best working properties and color for this
technique, but which is prone to cracking
throughout the process, adds another level of
challenge to this already difficult approach.
The results of this struggle are well worth it,
however, as born out by the piece shown here.

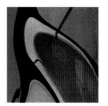

Formed of Fire

A FEAST FOR THE EYES

LAMPWORKED GLASS (sometimes also called flameworked glass) is one of the most dynamic branches of the studio glass movement. Underrated for many years as a medium for serious artists, lampworking has, in the last decade, exploded into the awareness of artists and collectors with a delightful variety of styles and techniques. In my own 27 years as a lampworker, I have witnessed this evolution firsthand: a virtuous cycle of innovation has stimulated the development of new tools, glass formulations and other technical advancements, which further encourages artists and craftsmen to experiment and stretch the envelope of lampworked glass.

Simply defined, lampwork is the craft of shaping glass in a torch flame. The traditional name derives from the original practice of melting glass rods and tubes in the flame of an oil lamp. In modern times, glassblowers use a gas-oxygen torch flame to heat their materials. As lampwork methods have become more popular, they have been incorporated and blended with other glass techniques. Nowadays, everything from tiny detailed renderings to massive architectural installations can be, and are, made by lampworking.

In this book, we will feast our eyes upon the creations of some of today's best lampwork artists, primarily from the United States. Their styles range from the elegant and sublime to the playful and funky. Many of these artists are self-taught; some have entered the world of studio lampwork indirectly, through apprenticeship with a traditional lampwork artisan or after training as a scientific glassblower. Whatever their origins, these artists have chosen to explore the possibilities of a challenging and delightful medium. Let's join them now in a visual feast of glass art.

LOREN STUMP
Kabuki, (Detail). *Photo: Rich Images.*

Lampworking, of all the arts with which I am acquainted, is the most agreeable and amusing: there is no object that cannot be made with enamels worked in the heat of the lamp, in only a few moments and more or less perfectly.

— DENIS DIDEROT

FOREWORD

ONE OF THE PRINCIPAL LITERARY achievements of the Age of Enlightenment was the monumental, 28-volume *Encyclopédie* edited by the French critic and philosopher Denis Diderot (1713–1784). It was published in parts from 1752 to 1771. The first work of its kind, the *Encyclopédie* was an attempt to collect and record all contemporary knowledge. In text and engravings, it described and depicted mechanical as well as craft processes, and lampworking—also called flameworking—was one of these documented activities.

Some 250 years after it was written, Diderot's commentary still rings true, but there have been many changes as well. The gas torch, patented in 1843, led to the rapid advancement of flameworking technology for both artistic and scientific purposes. (Before the invention of gas-fueled torches, the source of the lampworker's flame was an oil or paraffin lamp used in conjunction with foot-powered bellows.) In the late 1880s, Otto Schott invented borosilicate glass in Germany. Nearly 100 years later, this material was picked up by studio flameworkers, and the boundaries of flameworking with traditional soda-lime glass literally melted away.

The popularity of flameworking as a medium for art in glass has surged in the past five years. New artists, new techniques, and new applications abound. American studio flameworking, which encompasses a range of techniques rather than any single method, is undergoing an intensely creative period of the sort experienced in studio glassblowing in the 1980s. Much of this creativity is focused on developing and refining techniques. Innovative content is expanding at a slower rate, but as artists settle on new technical paths, I expect to see more sculptural and vessel-based work that not only draws from tradition, but is tradition-breaking.

Bandhu Scott Dunham's publications on lampworking are an invaluable resource for the artist, glass researcher, and glass enthusiast. This book presents an astoundingly diverse array of what can be accomplished with the flame. Flameworking can still be "agreeable and amusing," as Diderot observed, but Dunham shows us that flameworking today has the potential to express almost anything that an artist chooses to imagine.

TINA OLDKNOW
Curator of Modern Glass
The Corning Museum of Glass

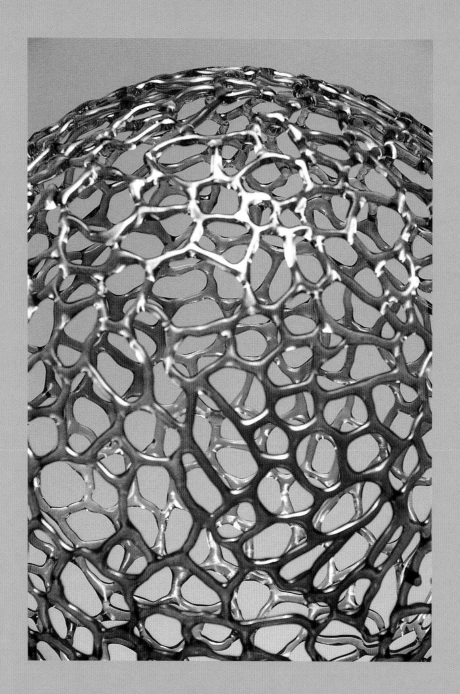

BANDHU DUNHAM
Rainbow Patchwork Aviary Sphere,
(Detail) *Photo: Courtesy of the Artist.*

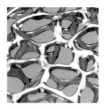

INTRODUCTION

LAMPWORK IS fascinating territory in the greater world of glass art. Its unique technical and aesthetic opportunities command the attention of a growing number of artists and appreciators around the globe. Every method of manipulating glass—whether "hot," "warm" or "cold"—brings out a different aspect of this amazing material. While lampworking shares some methods with other hot techniques, it is set apart by the primary use of a focused, directional heat source: the torch flame.

This makes a unique vocabulary of techniques available for detailed work. It also lends itself to the assembly of component pieces into larger objects. As Ginny Ruffner has pointed out, this gives lampwork a typically additive or linear quality. Artists using this technique are therefore challenged to make the best use of this quality, or to transcend it in an internal aesthetic confrontation.

By its nature, lampwork manipulates or alters glass that has previously been shaped by some other method. This is perhaps the foundation of that "additive" property of the technique. In this book, you will see how artists have taken tubes and rods and transformed them into the objects of their inspiration. In some cases the original form of the material is unrecognizable. In others, the starting shape has been allowed to assert itself, like white space on a page. This is just as true whether the raw glass was first shaped a moment earlier at the gaffer's bench or in the maw of a mechanical crucible at a far-away factory.

Lampwork, to my mind, is inherently clever in that it takes a given and does something else with it. This is fundamental to the artistic impulse, of course, but lampwork is perhaps uniquely blessed, among glass

above: **JOHN CHILES**
Goblet, 8 inches high. Combined furnace blown and lampworked technique. *Photo: May Mantel.*

right: **LOREN STUMP**
Murrini Paperweight, 4 inches diameter. Lampworked soda lime and lead glass. *Photo: Rich Images.*

techniques, in its ability to do this. Lampworkers are always taking things a step further, and we can perhaps see this in a kind of witticism that appears when lampwork methods are brought to bear on projects using other techniques. The artist seems to say "Ah, look, I can add more detail now," or "See, I can take a goblet and make it do *this.*"

One of my favorite things about lampwork is the way it bridges worlds. For example, the technique is ancient and traditional, but it has always been at the forefront of material culture. In ancient times, to shape glass at all required special furnaces that seemed magical (even demonic) to the common people. Early lampworking torches were similarly placed at the cutting edge of technology in their day. New techniques of scientific glassblowing, used to fabricate experimental apparatus for the advancement of technical knowledge, are often pressed into the service of art in novel ways, even today.

Lampwork has an ongoing relationship with science, more so than other glass fields. The first microscope lenses were formed by lampworking, and countless crucial developments in chemistry, physics and other sciences have depended on apparatus made of lampworked glass. The techniques and vocabulary of science are

therefore more familiar to branches of lampwork, and some lampworked glass can be seen as a dialogue between art and science. The development of neon and plasma sculpture is an excellent example of this conversation. While strict technical guidelines must be followed to make the enclosed gasses glow, the sensual, atmospheric luminosity that results makes it clear that creative inspiration

is in the driver's seat. Indeed, the sensuality of glass itself is responsible for seducing a number of technical glassblowers into the circle of craftsmen and artists. It is fun to try and guess an artist's background while looking at the lampworked glass throughout this book, although the true answers can be surprising.

Lampworking is also "contemporary" in its encouragement of an

individual approach to the medium. Although lampworkers can and do work together, the typical studio is a one-person operation. This gives free reign to the individual's creative inspiration and the development of a personal language. And while lampworking can be and is a spontaneous process, it also affords the artist an opportunity to readjust the form, to refine the embodiment of his inspiration, in a way that other hot glass forming methods do not.

Undeniably high-tech, lampworked glass is also high-touch. Although artists have sometimes felt uncomfortable with the "cute" associations traditionally given to lampworked glass, that very quality of smallness or intimacy can be a great strength and a resource on which to draw. The techniques of miniaturization and magnification available to the lampworker (as in mosaic cane work and paperweights) open unique worlds for exploration.

Beads and other ornamentation have always been formed by lampworking, giving an intimate highlight

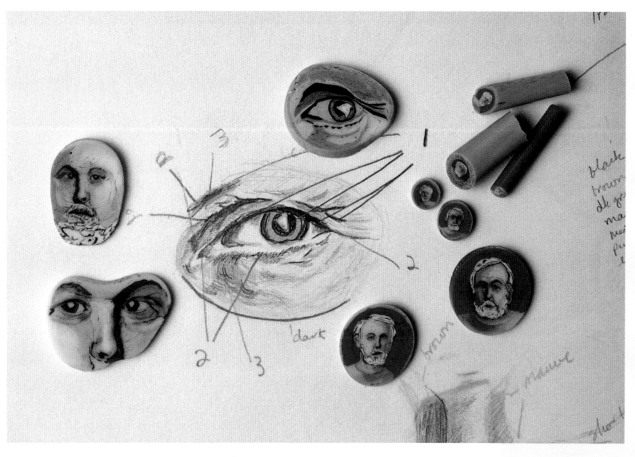

to the humanizing properties of glass. Using lampwork techniques, artists create remarkable virtual worlds within solidified drops of glass, whether as small as a tiny marble or as large as a composite casting. In the case of literal renderings, such as floral beads or paperweights, we are not only entertained, but also drawn to reflect on the beauty of Nature and possibly

to recall, on some level, our place in it. More abstract encasements, like we see in marbles and some jewelry, draw us into other kinds of reveries, dispelling for a moment the mundane limitations of our physical reality. In either case, we are brought into momentary contact with something essential, inspiring or universal within ourselves.

DINAH HULET
PS...A Portrait Study, Murrine canes and slices. Soda lime glass.
Photo: P. Hulet.

KIM WERTZ
Dragonfly and Encased Floral Bead,
Lampworked soda lime glass. Dragonfly:
7 cm wingspan. Bead: 5 cm long. *Photo:*
Greg Gallardy.

If the artist's job is to open our eyes to the mysterious and magical nature of human existence, then the glittering and enticing qualities of small lampworked objects are a delightful vehicle by which to accomplish that end. If that makes them "cute," so be it. In any case, lampwork is by no means limited to the creation of small objects, as the images in this volume attest. There are really no inherent limits to the scale, complexity or subtlety which can be achieved through lampworking today.

BEGINNINGS

THE EXACT ORIGINS of glass in general, and of lampwork technique in particular, are something of a mystery. We have no credible written records of a single brilliant inventor who came up with this clever method of manipulating an amazing material. Historians of ancient times have passed down fables, which are educational, but their standards of literal accuracy are different from our own.

The Roman historian Pliny, for example, tells us that glass was invented serendipitously by a crew of sailors, who made a fire on a beach one night using chunks of their cargo, the mineral *natron* (soda, or sodium carbonate) as a fire ring. The combination of sand (the main component of glass), a fluxing agent (soda) and heat produced the first glass.

While historians of our time don't give much credence to this so-called "campfire theory," it does rightly suggest that the first glass was accidental. Quite probably a crude glassy material was observed among the slag

WILLIAM MORRIS
Panther Comb, 10 inches high 11 inches wide 3 inches deep. Offhand blown and torch worked glass, steel stand. *Photo: Rob Vinnedge.*

from the smelting of metal ore, or perhaps as an offshoot of some artisan's work in ceramics or *faience*, an early glass-like material. In any event, trial and error was an important aspect of developing and refining the world's first man-made glasses. The first true lampwork is probably a collection of beads thought to date to the fifth century BC.

The journey from those beads to the dramatic lampwork of today (including beads, still!) is a long and fascinating one, about which I have written at length elsewhere. The primary focus of this book is contemporary lampworked glass, that is, lampwork which falls within or near the domain of the Studio Glass Movement, and for that matter, primarily work being done in the US. The specific origins of lampwork technique in this country are therefore of special interest.

We can identify several main "tracks" or threads running through the history of lampwork in America. One is the scientific or technical; others include the "novelty" glassblowers (who function as entertainers and produce wares suitable as gift items), as well as paperweight makers, beadmakers and artisans focusing on more avant-garde creative projects.

Scientific Glassblowing

Although the use of lampworking to create scientific apparatus dates back to at least the 17th century, the modern scientific lampworking industry was not born until the 1820s. It was then that a German professor of chemistry initiated the practice of including practical laboratory study in his courses, setting a precedent that was soon followed by his colleagues. This greatly increased the demand for

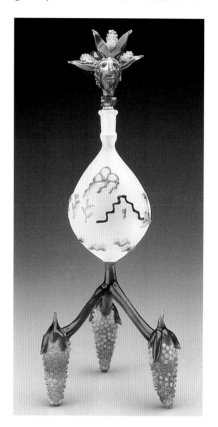

chemical apparatus, and the impetus of this demand established Germany as a leading global source of scientific apparatus until the outbreak of WWI.

By the turn of the 20th century, the development of practical borosilicate glass formulas made great advances in chemical apparatus possible. This class of glasses resists thermal shock and chemical attack, making them ideal for fabricating complex scientific contraptions. Corning Glass Works released their own version of borosilicate glass (commonly known as "7740" or Pyrex™) in time to meet the demand for apparatus in this country when the Great War eliminated the supply from Germany.

Happily, the thermal-shock resistant properties of borosilicate glass also make it an excellent medium for complex sculptural work. The technical expertise of scientific glassblowers has therefore been indispensable in the development of contemporary lampworked art. In fact, there are a number of lampwork artists whose day job is the fabrication of scientific apparatus, an arrangement which enables them to keep body and soul together while honing their skills with the medium they love. Other artists simply make use of the techniques, components and equipment of the scientific glassblower to carry out their work.

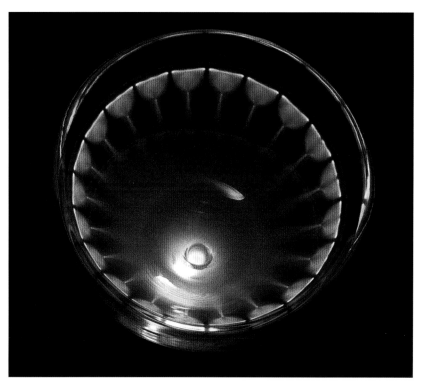

Luminous Sculpture

A kind of crossover was achieved between the technical and aesthetic during the later part of the 19th century. The Victorian era embodied, among other things, a fascination with bold new developments in science as well as a penchant for intricate ornamentation. These themes were married in the fanciful Geissler Tubes which were popular parlor toys/medical devices in the mid to late 1800s. Predecessors to neon illumination,

these sealed glass tubes contained gasses which lit up when excited by an electrical current. The resulting "radiant matter" was considered beneficial to one's health, and what's more, the elaborate luminous curlicues were beautiful to behold. Some modern plasma sculptures created "at the lamp" pay obvious homage to these charming devices, but all owe their origins to the techniques developed to make them.

Commercially viable neon signs began to appear after 1910, when tech-

nological advances made purified noble gasses and durable electrodes possible. Neon became extremely popular as a means of advertising up until the 1960s when the increasing use of backlit plastic signage reduced the demand. Since 1980, however, neon has made a big comeback in the commercial arena, and has been used increasingly by artists for its purity of line and color. While all neon sign bending is technically a form of lampwork, we are especially delighted by tubes that have been used sculpturally,

far left:
HARALD W. EBERHART
Spirus, 12 inches high 4 inches wide 4 inches deep Three-dimensional neon/argon plasma sculpture in borosilicate glass. *Photo: Kurt F. Seefeldt.*

left:
EDWARD KIRSHNER
Cone of Chaos, 12 inches high 8 inches wide 8 inches deep Double-walled glass form with neon gas plasma. *Photo: Courtesy of the Artist.*

"'Cone of Chaos' investigates the principles of a developing concept in physics, that of self-organizing chaos.

"What appears as a simple formal grace to the work is actually the result of exhaustive fine-tuning. I spend days, weeks, even months in planning, designing, and manipulating variables and still the plasma behaves in a way I can never completely control. I can change or direct its behavior, by changing the pressure and mix of the gases or the frequency and voltage of the power, but I can not fully predict what effect my actions will have on the plasma. Though frustrating at times, this unpredictability is at the heart of the work. This is the mystery and life I strive to produce in my sculpture."

right:

Apple Blossom. Rudolph and Leopold Blaschka, *courtesy of the Botanical Museum of Harvard University, Cambridge, MA.* (Life size).

far right:

MARGARET NEHER

Cattleya Scent Bottle, 6 inches high. Lampworked borosilicate glass. *Photo: Dan Neuberger.*

"I'm fascinated by the endless variety of shapes and colors found in nature, and in orchids in particular. At the same time, I find myself frustrated by their ephemeral nature. I think this is why I've always been drawn to realism in my work; to the challenge of working to capture a complex, ever-changing living thing in an unchanging form. Lampworked glass is particularly suited to this. The fluidity of the process allows the piece to keep evolving..."

bottom right:

Paul Stankard *prepares the components of a paperweight for encasement by the vacuum technique. Photo: James Amos.*

modified at the torch, or made into free-standing plasma sculptures, which can operate without the need for electrodes. Such luminous creations are the most high-tech expression of lampworking's ongoing relationship with science. Other works incorporate furnace blown bubbles or found glass objects, with lampwork playing an important but less visible role in the assembly.

Reflections of Nature

Also reflecting a melding of the aesthetic and scientific were glass models of various plants and animals that came into use in the mid 19th century. The most famous of these are the Blaschka Glass Flowers commissioned for Harvard University in 1887. Produced by a father/son team in Germany, these remarkable specimens, comprising thousands of models, have recently benefited from a major renovation of their display and can still be seen at the Harvard Botanical Museum in Cambridge, Massachusetts. Another famous maker of models was Herman O. Mueller, who made astonishing replicas of microorganisms in glass for the American Museum of Natural History in New York City during the middle of the 20th century.

Related to the making of models, but leaning more into the realm of pure aesthetics is the world of paperweights. The paperweight as we know it seems to have appeared almost simultaneously in France, Italy and Germany in the mid-1840s. American factories began producing them within ten years, and paperweights have been popular collector's items ever since. Since the birth of the Studio Glass Movement, artists like Paul Stankard and Victor Trabucco have brought these to new heights, even outgrowing the term "paperweight." The technique of vacuum encasement, originally developed for making paperweights has also been embraced by lampworkers for the making of marbles and more complex sculpture.

In general, figurative renderings and models have always been a fertile field of creative exploration, entertainment and contemplation. The traditions of lampworked figurines go back at least as far as the Nevers figures which originated in seventeenth century France. Such miniatures were the playthings of the wealthy, including Louis XIII, as well as objects of adoration when incorporated in religious compositions.

Early in the current renaissance of public recognition, some lampworkers felt the need to distance our contemporary work from the more

above:
VICTOR TRABUCCO
Swallowtail, 4 inches diameter. Lampworked glass, cold worked. *Photo: Courtesy of the Artist.*

left:
Holy Water Font, 18th century, probably Nevers, France. 23 cm high, 12.4 cm wide. *Courtesy of the Juliette K. and Leonard S. Rakow Research Library of the Corning Museum of Glass.*

top right:

VITTORIO CONSTANTINI

Long Life Japanese Cranes, 14 cm high, tallest. Lampworked soda-lime glass. *Photo: Gianni Lapenna—Venice.*

top far right:

BERNARD & SOKOLOFF

Fierce Martini—Black Tip Shark,
9 inches high 4.5 inches wide 4.5 inches deep. Flameworked blown and sculpted borosilicate glass. *Photo: Dennis Tannen*

"The way we challenge ourselves and handle the frustrations that we encounter is by immersing combined talents into glass. This is an experience in problem solving which results in immense gratification and a sense of accomplishment for us."

bottom right:

SHANE FERO

Madame Magritte, 16 inches high 8.5 inches wide 8.5 inches deep. Flameworked borosilicate glass, plate glass base. Sandblasted. *Photo: John Littleton.*

bottom far right:

KAREN BUHLER

A Morning Shower, 22 inches high 12 inches wide 4 inches deep. Lampworked borosilicate tube, lustered, sandblasted, cameo luster. *Photo: Russel Johnson.*

familiar figurative artisanal traditions. While this concern was understandable, for some it was simply not an issue. These practitioners of lampwork have instead taken figurative representation to new heights—either of representational detail, gestural quality or technical virtuosity. For such artists, the figure—whether human, animal or even botanical—represents a challenging context in which to hone or express their skill and enjoyment as a lampworker. Figurative work can be interpreted both as an honoring reference to and an extension of, a craft tradition that goes back centuries.

Novelty, Folk and Humor

When lampworking first asserted itself on the radar screens of the Studio Glass Movement, most artists took great pains to distinguish their use of lampwork from the more familiar novelty makers at county fairs and shopping malls. It was difficult to draw serious attention to contemporary lampwork when most people's image of the technique was adrift on a sea of spun-glass sailing ships or wedded to a sentimental cake top. Novelty lampwork was considered something of an embarrassment to more serious artists, because we always had to explain ourselves in reaction to

people's familiarity with the traditional novelties. Now that we have come into our own, lampworkers can be a little more relaxed about the supposed skeletons in our closet. The fact is that we owe a debt of gratitude to the hardworking artisans who kept the technical traditions of lampwork alive. It is even possible that by now we might be able to relax and not take ourselves too seriously!

A tradition of itinerant lampworkers was well-established in Europe before the time of the American Revolution. The equipment of that time was quite different from the gasoxygen torches used by lampworkers today. The heat for shaping the glass was provided by a sort of oil lamp (hence the term "lampworking"), with

above:
SCOTT BISSON
Skinks, 7 inches wide overall.
Flameworked borosilicate glass
Photo: Shadowsmith.

top far left:
EMILIO SANTINI
Acquatica, 11 inches high 17 inches wide. Cast glass with lampworked inclusions. *Photo: Dixon.*

bottom far left:
PAT OWENS
Destinations, 10.5 inches high 13.75 inches wide 10.5 inches deep. Lampworked soda lime glass, enameled plate glass, patinated bronze casting. *Photo: Courtesy of the Artist.*

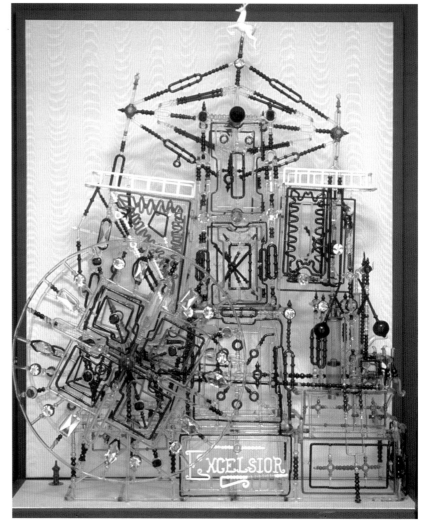

a jet of air injected into the flame to augment the temperature. The flow of air was supplied by a foot-operated bellows, requiring a good set of leg muscles. Some artisans would travel from town to town, offering demonstrations of their craft and products for sale, including miniature figurines.

Immigrants brought that tradition to this country, and here it evolved, by the mid-nineteenth century, to include large "troupes" of traveling glassblowers, often related by blood. These glassblowing families became lineages, a few of which survive even into this day, although the extravagant road shows of the Victorian times are a thing of the past.

The typical performance in the late 1800s consisted of one to fifteen lampworkers demonstrating their trade in a variety of forms. An empty storefront might be rented for a few days, or in some cases a longer period. Spectators were lured into the show by dramatic broadsides promising an educational demonstration of the most advanced glass wizardry. Contests

were sometimes held and prizes awarded to the prettiest girl in the audience or the man with the biggest nose. Demonstrations included the pulling of glass fibers (spun onto a large wheel), Cartesian divers (or "bottle imps," which seemed to swim magically in a tank of water), the crafting of glass figurines and audience participation stunts. Especially interesting were the working model steam engines created by some of the troupes. The sensibility of the time was very open to demonstrations that were both educational and entertaining. The sense of wonder at the leaps and bounds of the natural sciences and Machine Age technology at this time was amplified by the beauty of the glass artistry.

Because the various troupes of lampworkers considered each other competition, and because an air of magic enhanced the caché of their performances, a tradition of secrecy developed among the glassblowing families in the US. This meant that it was difficult to learn the technique except by committing oneself to a long apprenticeship within one of the family lineages. It was perhaps due to this secrecy that the lampworking families diminished over time, the performances devolving into much smaller and more sedentary affairs.

above:
JENI & DEL WOOCK
People Perfume, 6 inches high
Lampworked glass, mixed media.
Photo: George Post.

top far left:
NANCY NAGEL
By the Light of the Moon, 8 inches high 12 inches wide 12 inches deep
Lampworked and cast glass. *Photo: David Harrison.*

bottom left:
FREDERICK BIRKHILL
Flagellate Goblet Fantasy, 12 inches high, tallest. Lampworked soda-lime and lead glasses. *Photo: Courtesy of the Artist.*

right:

SHARON PETERS

Lizardos di Caprio, 4 inches high 3 inches wide 1.5 inches deep. Compound beads; lampworked soda lime glass. *Photo: Janice Peacock.*

"Most of my designs are bright and goofy, because I like that kind of thing. My first sculptural beads were remakes in glass of designs I'd been doing since I was a kid, and now they come out of my cartoons and doodles. The primary tools that I use for sculptural work are an x-acto/utility bladed tool, the warm ends of thin glass rods, and gravity."

far right:

LOREN STUMP

OJ Chase Scene, 4 inches diameter. Lampworked, vacuum encased assembly. *Photo: Rich Images.*

One of the modern masters of murrine fabrication, Loren Stump adds ever finer levels of detail to his creations. In this darkly whimsical recreation of an historic moment for American media, a close inspection reveals extraordinary touches on the police cars, and (not shown here) even the face of the fugitive suspect inside the lead vehicle.

The lone lampworker spinning novelties at the shopping mall is the most familiar example of the latter end of this tradition in America, although vibrant strands of creativity do still come from this direction. It was only in the latter part of the twentieth century that the "Glass Curtain" of family secrecy really began breaking down, allowing an influx of new blood into the traditional artisan niche. This greater openness has also helped fuel the expansion of lampwork within the Studio Glass Movement, and members of the lampworking families that still exist have both taken advantage of this creative opportunity and been a valuable source of technical expertise for many artists.

We can also observe a modern folk-lampworking tradition developing in small independent workshops around the US. Young men and women are learning the techniques of lampwork and applying them to the production of jewelry, marbles, musical instruments, tobacco pipes and other functional objects. Still in its early stages, this movement remains limited in its stylistic range, but increasing numbers of skilled and talented lampworkers are rising out of this potentially fertile field of experimentation.

One could also argue that a certain element of humor in lampwork can be traced to folk or artisanal traditions. Ordinary objects made extraordinary by a comical twist are sometimes the result of repetitive or simply playful familiarity. They certainly benefit from an environment in which the creator does not take herself too seriously and a viewer might be half-expecting a form of entertainment.

Some lampworkers—not unlike the glass factory workers, going back centuries, who would take a moment out of their day to create "whimsies" such as glass hats, walking canes or trick goblets—can't turn down the chance for a laugh. And what better medium than lampwork to create witticisms to make our own eyes sparkle? As in the greater art world, the humor of lampworkers ranges from the truly light-hearted to the darkly funny. Make no mistake about the level of skill needed to execute these pieces, however. They may or may not be "serious" art, but they represent a serious commitment to developing a nuanced technique and a respect for the material.

Beads and Marbles

Lampwork beadmaking is a tradition dating from at least the fifth century BC. The first lampworked objects are believed to be beads, and while the craft never died out completely, the advent of mechanical production (and probably other factors) drew attention away from handmade glass beads until a more recent renaissance. Twenty years ago, no one could have foreseen the tremendous impact that glass beadmaking was to have in the world of American crafts. From

humble beginnings, there has grown a contemporary glass bead movement of remarkable proportions. Hundreds of beadmakers are actively working across this country, producing everything from simple decorative accents to elaborate sculptural beads that dazzle and captivate the eye. Tiny worlds unto themselves, beads have a very long tradition. The rich vocabulary of historical reference this affords combines with technical opportunities unavailable until only recently to bring us a staggering variety of amazing beads. Incorporated into larger works like necklaces or sculpture, or as stand-alone objects, beads are a very satisfying field of exploration both for artists and art appreciators. A significant proportion of contemporary lampwork artists first sat down at the

torch to make beads, and while many have turned their attention to other aspects of lampworking, a good number have continued to explore mandrel wound beads, taking them in interesting directions and to new heights.

Marbles, like paperweights, have long been highly collectible. This specialty has not been neglected as lampwork has expanded in the last 15 years, so that there are more lampworkers producing collectible marbles than ever before.

The Studio Glass Movement

Originating from the experimental workshops mounted by Harvey Littleton and Dominick Labino in the early 1960s, the Studio Glass Movement has become a significant feature of America's artistic landscape. One

above:
MARCO JERMAN
Double Latticinio, 1.75 inches diameter
Lampworked borosilicate glass.
Photo: Jim King/Royal Images.

left:
ALETHIA DONATHAN
Pen and Letter Opener, 5.5 inches
long. Lampworked and coldworked glass
with metal inserts. *Photo: Masayo Suzuki.*

above:
KRISTEN FRANTZEN ORR
Floral Tapestry Beads, 5.4 cm high
tallest Lampworked soda-lime glass.
Photo: Dave Orr.

top right:
PHYLLIS CLARKE
Fox and Japanese Macaque Beads,
1.25 inches high, tallest. Lampworked
soda-lime glass. *Photo: Robert Liu.*

bottom right:
AMY HAFTKOWYCZ
Collection of Borosilicate Beads,
1 inch high. 6 inches wide 6 inches deep
overall. Lampworked, mandrel-wound.
Photo: Steve Waskow.

of the most commonly cited defining features of this movement is the possibility for individual artists to work with hot glass outside of a factory setting. Lampwork would seem to fit right into this definition from the beginning, but for reasons mentioned earlier, lampwork was initially relegated, in many people's mind, to a kind of "outsider" status. This was a source of continual consternation and sometimes amusement for lampwork artists. At a Glass Art Society conference as late as 1996, a presentation focusing on international developments in lampwork, was half-jokingly titled, "Lampwork, The Red-Haired Cousin of the Studio Glass Movement."

A small number of talented and persistent artists can be credited with breaking through the glass ceiling that hung over lampwork. The foremost among them is Ginny Ruffner, whose unapologetically bold work quickly gained wide respect within the glass art establishment and brought the possibilities of lampwork to the forefront of people's attention. Paul Stankard, who began his apprenticeship to the craft as a scientific glassblower, developed a refinement of technique and sensibility that commanded the respect of collectors and critics worldwide. Shane Fero, who as a young man braved a traditional apprenticeship with a glassblowing family, was

also instrumental in raising the status of lampwork technique. Along with Fred Birkhill, an artist steeped in the lampwork traditions of Europe, Shane has taught hundreds of students, many of whom have become respected artists today. Sally Prasch also took what she gained in a traditional apprenticeship and shared it with students. Soon it was possible for more American lampworkers to receive the attention their work deserved, and the names of Brian Kerkvliet, Roger Parramore, Robert Mickelsen, and others became familiar to appreciators of glass art. In this book, you will see the work of many more established and emerging artists.

International Influences

Like the rest of the American Studio Glass Movement, contemporary lampwork has been invigorated by the infusion of techniques from Europe in recent years. Artists from Italy and Germany have taught lampwork technique in the US, and some have even migrated here to live and work. Artists like Césare Toffolo, Emilio Santini, Gianni Toso, Kurt Wallstab and others have generously shared their talents and techniques with eager American students. The effect has been to refresh the traditions of lampwork that were first brought over by itinerant artisans in the 18th and 19th centuries,

top far left:

SUSAN BREEN SILVY

Happy Life Lampwork Bead Bracelet, 7.5 inches long overall. Silver core lampworked beads, sterling silver. *Photo: Jeff O'Dell.*

"I love working with the fluidity of molten glass. It has its own life. While the artistic direction is mine, the personality of the glass also leaves its mark. Each bead is an individual work of art, no two beads can ever be exactly the same, each has its own personality and character."

top left:

REGINA WALLSTAB-BREITWIESER

Necklace,, 45 cm long overall. Lampworked glass, rock crystal. *Photo: Courtesy of the Artist.*

bottom left:

DEBBIE CROWLEY

Fish Bead Group, Lampworked soda lime glass. From left: "Hollow Spotted Puffer," 1.5 inches x 2 inches; "Clown Fish," 1.3 inches x 3.5 inches; "Blue Banded Butterfly Fish," 2.25 inches x 2,88. inches *Photo: Courtesy of the Artist.*

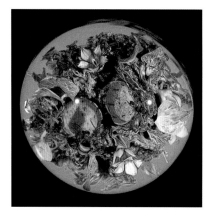

top right:
PAUL J. STANKARD
Red Fruit Bouquet with Mask, 3.25
inches diameter. Flameworked, kiln-cast,
cold worked glass. *Photo: James Amos.*

bottom right:
KAREN OVINGTON
Bottle Form, 3 inches high .75 inch
wide .75 inch deep. Lampworked glass,
sterling silver, pearl. *Photo: Tom Van
Enyde .*

Karen Ovington's use of surface etching,
rough powders and patinas enhance the
artifact-like quality of this small idiosyn-
cratic form. Part talisman, part ritual
vessel, it seems somehow familiar but
decidedly from another time or place.

far right:
SALLY PRASCH
Splash, 12 inches high 12 inches wide
12 inches deep. Lampworked borosilicate
glass. *Photo: Tommy Olaf Elder.*

while supporting the development of
a truly modern sensibility. Japanese
influences, especially in beadmaking
and core-forming techniques, are also
enriching our melting pot.

Into the 21st Century

Beauty, which was regarded with
suspicion during much of the 20th century, has been making a comeback
lately. It is even possible that self-
involved theoretical cleverness and
irony in art are going out of fashion,
if only temporarily. The sensual
delightfulness of glass, once regarded
as a liability during the debates about
"art" versus "craft" in the '80s is, more
and more, simply accepted as the
blessing—and challenge—it is. Exactly
where artists will go with these new

developments is hard to predict.

It may not be too early to say that in this new millennium, the technical and aesthetic possibilities of lampwork in particular are expanding beyond limits (real and imagined) which were in place for centuries. There is an unprecedented commingling of influences from all around the world, as well as new technologies, materials and artistic concerns.

The goals expressed by many lampworkers 20 years ago are starting to be achieved. There is no longer any significant stigma attached to our technique of choice, and the fact of being a lampworker, in and of itself, cannot be said to prevent success in the art market place. No school with

a glass curriculum is complete without a lampworking program, and no one who appreciates glass can go long without encountering, and falling in love with, the remarkable fruits of lampwork technique.

Glass, this ancient and wonderful material, continues to reveal new opportunities, both technically and aesthetically, to new generations of daring artists. Here then, is a tasty sampling from this remarkable movement within the world of Studio Glass. The delicious images which follow are a tribute to the ingenuity and vision of some of our best cultural resources— often spicy, sometimes sweet, but always a feast for the eyes!

Additional Reading:

Dunham, Bandhu, *Contemporary Lampworking: A Practical Guide to Shaping Glass in the Flame*, third edition, (Prescott, AZ: Salusa Glassworks, Inc., 2002).

Lierke, Rosemarie, "Early History of Lampwork—Some Facts, Findings and Theories, Part 2," *Glastechnische Berichte*, December, 1992.

Leier, et. al., *Contemporary Glass: Color, Light & Form,* (Madison, WI: Guild Publishing, 2001).

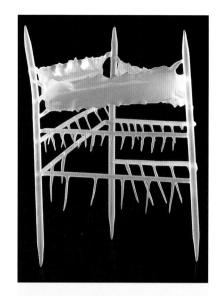

above:
GINNY RUFFNER
Dancing Box, 1983, 27 inches high 17 inches wide 17 inches deep. Lampworked borosilicate glass, sandblasted. *Photo: Courtesy of the Artist.*

left:
Césare Toffolo demonstrates the popularity of lampworking—*as well as his extraordinary technique—during the Glass Art Society Conference held in Corning, New York in 2001. He is in a white shirt, barely visible above the left shoulder of the black shirt near the center of the photo. Courtesy of the Studio of the Corning Museum of Glass.*

LOY ALLEN

above:
Fruit Scents, 7 inches high each. Borosilicate *glass. Photo: Sid Spelts.*

right:
Orchids, 12 inches high overall. Borosilicate glass and sandstone. *Photo: Sid Spelts.*

Loy Allen's lyrical plant forms are complemented by the rough sandstone of her native South Dakota. The combination of glass and stone completes a circle that begins with the raw mineral materials that are fused into glass. Like her whimsical perfume bottles, also inspired by nature, they conjure a harmony between animal, mineral and vegetable.

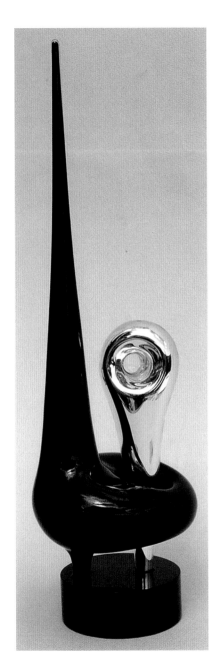

above:

Miniatures, 5 - 7 cm high each. Borosilicate glass, with metallic solutions applied prior to and during heating and manipulation of the glass. *Photo: Courtesy of the Artist.*

left:

Untitled, 31 cm high. Lampworked borosilicate glass, treated inside with hot bitomenic compounds and silver plating solutions. *Photo: Courtesy of the Artist.*

"I live and work in this area of the Mediterranen believed to be the origin of glass. The objects I create are lamp-blown glass, fused and patinated with metallic substances.

"I do not produce replicas of ancient glass, but it is only natural that my work should reflect designs which have their roots in this environment.... My sculptures are a dialogue with the fluid material, which frequently carries me away from, or beyond the original idea, and allows me, at my advanced age, the joy of play, discovery and creativity."

ALEX ARBELL

RICK AYOTTE

above:
Rose Bowl, 16 inches diameter, 16 inches high. *Photo: Melissa Ayotte.*

inset:
Rose Bowl, (alternate view) *Photo: Melissa Ayotte.*

RICK AYOTTE

right:
Floral Paperweight, 5.5 inches diameter 3 inches high. Encased lampwork. *Photo: Melissa Ayotte.*

Dramatic visual depth and startling realism characterize the floral paperweights of Rick Ayotte. Refining traditional techniques to a superb level, he creates simple compositions with meticulous attention to detail.

MICHAEL BARLEY

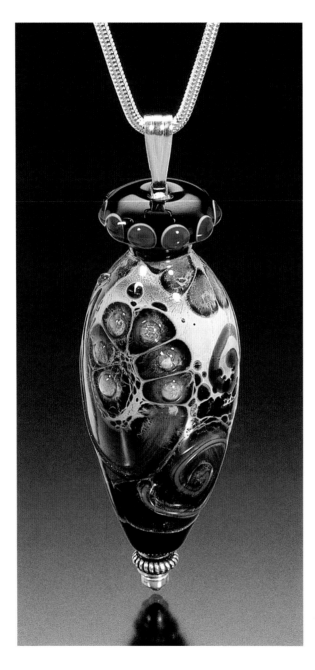

right:

Vessel Bead Pendant, 2.5 inches long.
Lampworked glass; mandrel-wound. *Photo: Doug Yaple.*

far right:

Vessel Bead Pendant, 2.5 inches long
Lampworked glass; mandrel-wound *Photo: Doug Yaple.*

Michael Barley's richly decorated vessel pendants echo an ancient tradition of beads with a vessel form. Brought up to date with a contemporary color pallette and fittings, they still evoke their roots in primal decorative patterns and a mystical depth of imagery possible only in glass which has been applied in successive layers.

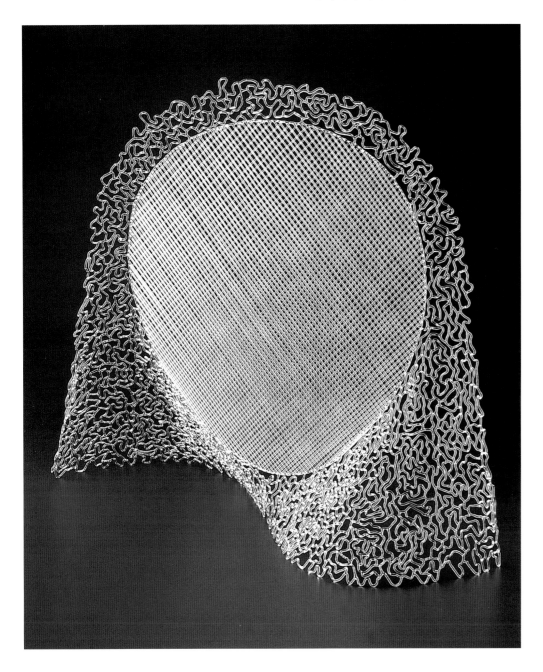

above:

Rope Trick, 14 inches high 14 inches wide 7 inches deep, Flameworked glass rod. *Photo: Bill Bachhuber.*

left:

Hoop Work, 25 inches high 21 inches wide 14 inches deep. Flameworked glass rod. *Photo: Bill Bachhuber.*

"Usually my pieces start out from a mathematical idea, but 'Hoop Work' started with a bar of soap. The soap shape is abstracted a bit here; its' the straight rods in the middle. For me the piece has lots of mathematical richness even though it didn't start that way. It touches on some nice symmetries and paper-folding problems, and I like the way the lens manages to have thickness in spite of being just straight lines across a loop. There was an unexpected bonus: If you look at it from a certain distance your eyes get physically uncomfortable from trying to focus on it. It's good; a visual equivalent of hot pepper.

"I make all my pieces in mid-air freehand, one bend at a time. Slumping and molds don't work for the sorts of shapes I like to make. I admit it's a little frivolous to work in a medium in which signing my initials takes half an hour—or for that matter to make pieces which can be broken with a feather duster. Luckily, even with some spectacular accidents, so far all the breaks have been easily reparable. Glass is a surprisingly resilient substance; another reason I like working with it."

FREDERICK BIRKHILL

above:

Biomorphic Cylinder, 5 inches high 2 inches diameter. Lampworked lead glass. *Photo: Courtesy of the Artist.*

"My sources of ideas are numerous, ranging from imagery derived from nature to a romantic belief in a European tradition of glass art. Much of my current work is based on Surrealistic imagery using mixed media in conjunction with glass."

right:

Arboreal Goblets, 9 inches high, tallest. Painted enamels on lampworked glass. *Photo: Courtesy of the Artist.*

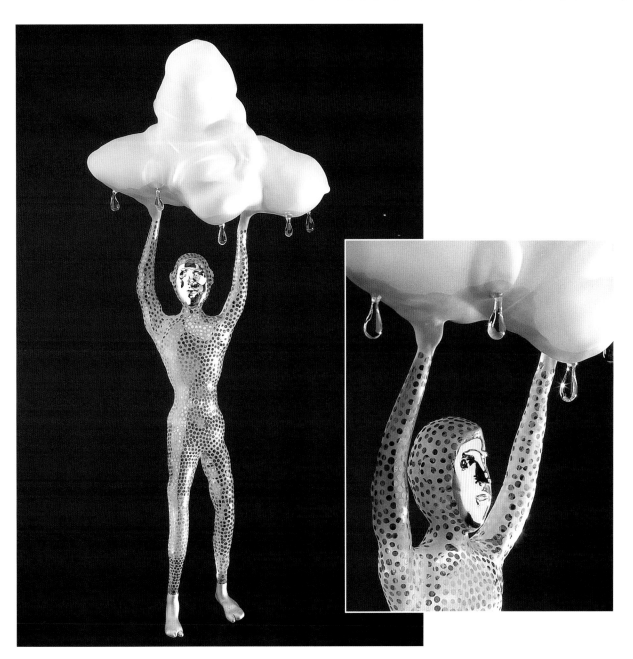

Partly Cloudy, 20 inches high 8 inches wide 3 inches deep. Wall mounted piece. Lampworked borosilicate glass, sandblasted. *Photo: Russel Johnson* .

inset:
Partly Cloudy, (Detail) *Photo: Russel Johnson.*

"This colorful, godlike man can be seen as holding or hanging from a raincloud. This piece reflects the affects and effects of weather.

"It's magical when I transform four-foot sticks of glass into sculpture while seated at the controls of a Zenit bench burner. Lampworking glass fills me with a sense of accomplishment and integrity and has proven over time to be my vehicle of expression, of translating inner vision to outer reality. Besides that, it's fun.

"Cloudpeople are blown from many sections of tube. Each section is blown and shaped; then sealed to another blown and shaped tube. One sculpture may have 20 tube parts before it is completed as one hollow form. It is a fascinating process. They are lightweight, almost floating yet strong. They are action figures or dolls, god-like, in skinsuits, effecting or being affected by the weather/mood/spirit of the billowing cloud above.

"Borosilicate is my glass of choice because it is so thermally forgiving and can be modeled into any form imaginable. Manipulating it in the bench burner and kiln allows me to work quickly and spontaneously. Annealing, cooling, and assembling can be done many times in a session. The piece can be changed and rearranged if needed throughout the process. Although other artists have struggled with the many limits of borosilicate, I have found it to be most responsive to my process and forms of expression."

ELLIE BURKE

Cladaugh Necklace, 2.75 inches high 3
inches wide 1 inch deep. Influenced by Irish
Friendship Necklace design; flameworked
center. 24 inches long overall. *Photo:
William F. Lemke.*

ELLIE BURKE

Moving Forward, 11 inches high 30 inches wide 12 inches deep. Flameworked borosilicate glass and mixed media. *Photo: William F. Lemke.*

"I love the immediacy of flameworking. I will make components and later assemble them into a larger piece. The best part about the sculptural work is that I can get absorbed in the process and forget about time. They become meditations. Meditations on my family, my health and environment, and pop-culture. And because they are deeply rooted in a personal episode, they have a life of their own that other people respond to."

RON CARLSON

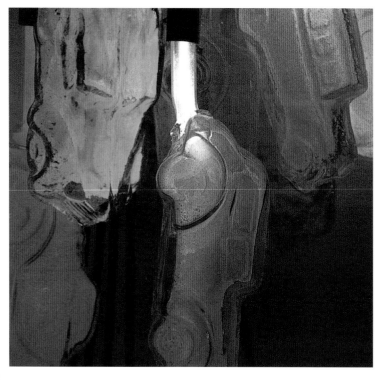

above:
Diesel Bouquet, (Detail) *Photo: Chris Nodland.*

right:
Diesel Bouquet, 48 inches high 12 inches wide
12 inches deep. Mold-blown hot glass, filled with
krypton. *Photo: Chris Nodland.*

Ron Carlson directs the Crafts Center at the
University of California, San Diego. Combining
lampworking and furnace blowing techniques, he
gathers molten glass on the end of a neon tube,
which serves as a blowpipe. After annealing, an
electrode is sealed onto the blown form using a
torch. The cars, trucks and buses have been phos-
phored inside, and colored glass was used in some
cases.

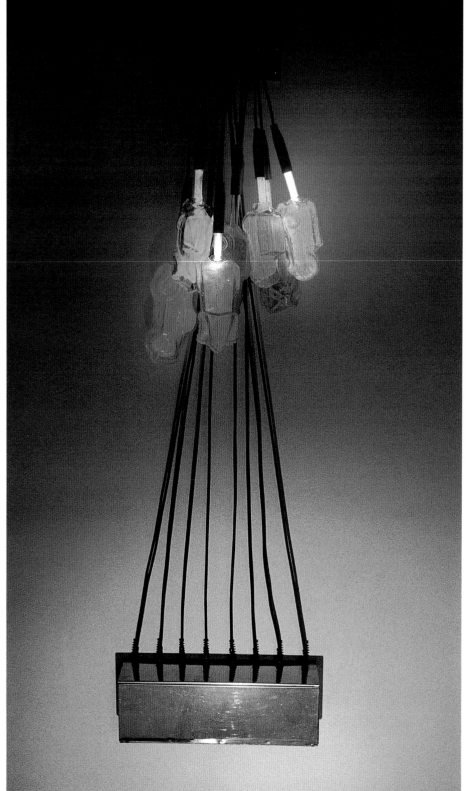

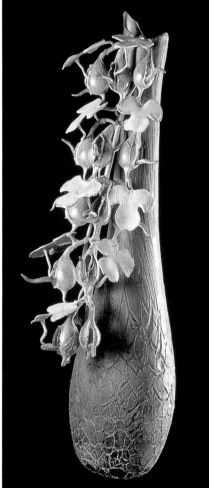

VICTOR CHIARIZIA

left:

My Father's Figs, 21 inches high 6 wide
6 deep. Lampworked and blown glass.
Photo: Holly Augeri.

far left:

The Magic of a Maker's Hands,
19 inches high 8 inches wide 8 inches deep.
Lampworked, blown and sand-carved glass,
pate de verre. *Photo: Holly Augeri.*

*"In my newest work, I look deeply to the
human experience and my own life for
inspiration. Each sculpture tells a unique
story: the joy and agony of the artist's soul,
a question asked and perhaps answered,
death, new beginnings, fond memories, a
dream realized or one yet to be. I invite the
viewer to draw their own conclusions from
that which speaks to their soul."*

JOHN CHILES

above:

Organic Bottles, 11.5 inches high, tallest. Furnace blown bottles with lampworked elements in the stoppers. *Photo: May Mantel.*

right:

Goblet Grouping, 10 inches high. Furnace blown and lampworked glass. *Photo: May Mantel.*

"I generally use multiple elements in the design and construction of my pieces. The hot torch is an integral part of my process at the glass blowing bench for both shaping elements and spot heating them before joining."

above:

Scarlet Tanager Teapot, 8 inches high 8 inches wide 3 inches deep.
Lampworked soda-lime glass. *Photo: Richard Clarke.*

left:

Calico Cat, **Queen Angelfish and Cardinal Vessels,** 8.5 inches high 2.5 inches
wide 2.5 inches deep. Lampworked soda-lime glass. *Photo: Richard Clarke.*

*"The purpose of my quest is to develop a relationship to my work…in the
process of creation, I explore the subject matter of my pieces and the medium
in which I work. Animals have always been my teachers and guides throughout life and through honoring them, I strive to access the creativity I was
blessed with and learn to express it in a form that is worthy of the inspiration.*

*"I believe that each artist who works with diligence and sincerity and strives
to form a unique and intimate relationship with the piece that is in the flame
at the moment will ultimately be able to come to an understanding with
themselves and the source of all creativity in the universe."*

RICHARD CLEMENTS

above:

Vases, 7 inches high. Lampworked borosilicate glass. *Photo: Allen Moult.*

right:

Tea Pot with Cozy, 6 inches high 6 inches wide 6 inches deep. Lampworked borosilicate glass. *Photo: Allen Moult.*

Frustrated with the difficulty of obtaining commercial colored borosilicate glass in his native Tasmania, Richard Clements developed his own formulas and now produces them in small batches for his own use (as well as occasional sale to other artists). In addition to a unique color pallette, his work manifests an underlying witticism which is nicely complemented by the qualities of lampworked glass.

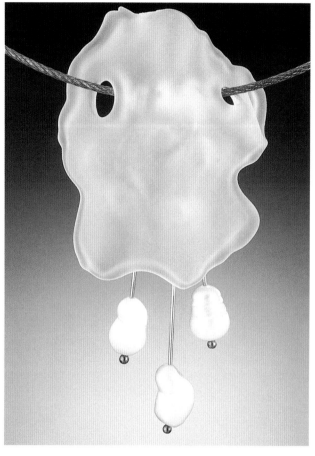

ELOISE COTTON

above:

Abstraction, 1.5 inches high. Lampworked glass, sandblasted; mixed media. Inspired by the work of Elizabeth Mears. *Photo: Hap Sakwa.*

left:

Emergence, 1.5 inches long. Flameworked glass, sandblasted; mixed media. *Photo: Hap Sakwa.*

Eloise Cotton's elegant compositions shown here rely on simply stated and subtle contrasts of form, color and surface. Allowing the opened borosilicate tubing to speak with its own voice, she engages in a conversation with the material which is natural in mood.

VITTORIO CONSTANTINI

School of Tropical Fishes,
10 cm long each.
Lampworked soda-lime
glass. *Photo: Gianni Lapenna
—Venice.*

Vittorio Constantini demonstrates the steps in making one of his extraordinary fish during the Glass Art Society conference in Amsterdam, 2002. Here he has begun shaping the body from a prepared color assembly to which he has applied layers of clear glass.

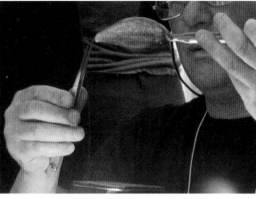

As Constantini stretches the body, you can see its general shape.

Clear glass is applied to form the tail and fins.

Tweezers are used to give realistic texture to the fins.

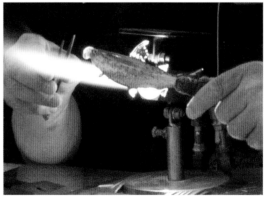

Now he grasps the fish by the tail, removes the glass rod which had served as a handle, and forms the mouth.

The completed fish, ready for the annealer.

GISELLE COURTNEY

above:

Water Pod Choker, 40 cm long overall. Lampworked borosilicate glass, copper electroformed, silver plated. *Photo: Rowan Fotheringham.*

right:

Anemone, 35 cm high 25 cm wide 15 cm deep. Lampworked borosilicate glass, electroformed copper, 24kt gold plate. *Photo: Paul Green.*

"In Australia, most of us live by the coast, therefore our coastline is an integral part of our personal geography ensuring even the busiest section of the community has time to pause and reflect, however briefly, on the water and its continually changing form. This constant change of water and light, has inspired my art and driven me to make glass sculpture and jewelry that is designed to enrich lives by reflecting the tones, colours, movement and history of its surroundings. My interest in borosilicate glass lies in its clarity and optically refractive qualities. Through its use as a medium, I have developed a way of capturing and throwing light unique in contemporary practice. Its inherent strength makes it perfect for both jewelry and public art. It allows me to realise my concepts by supporting the tiny myriad of surface details and textures that I achieve through thermal manipulation and sandblasting."

Dinnerware and Perfumes, 8 inches high overall. Lampworked glass and mixed media. *Photo: Paul Poplis.*

Donavon Boutz and Suzan Benzle draw from a family heritage of glass-blowing going back to the Columbian Exhibition of 1893 in this country, and before that to deeper roots among German glassblowing families from the Thuringerwald. These assorted functional wares use both borosilicate and the more challenging soda-lime glass popular in the Old World to bring a sophisticated sparkle to every day objects.

BANDHU DUNHAM

above:

Creeping Alchemical Gazing Bowl, 5 inches high 7 inches diameter Lampworked borosilicate glass. *Photo: Courtesy of the Artist.*

"In these bowls, I seek to balance contradicting forces: a simple visual richness, reflecting a mood of contemplation with a kinetic edge. The color effects are achieved through multiple layerings of glass powders, gold and silver fuming, clear trails, sandblasting and acid polishing—not necessarily in that order."

right:

Curly-Footed Gazing Bowl, 5 inches high 7 inches diameter. *Photo: Courtesy of the Artist.*

Rainbow Patchwork Aviary Sphere,
11 inches diameter. Lampworked and slumped
borosilicate glass; lustered. *Photo: Courtesy of
the Artist.*

*"My spheres are the result of extensive
technical experimentation and combine
lampworking with kiln techniques to
achieve the symmetrical form. As primor-
dially simple shapes with a surface full of
organic variation and irregularities, the
works of this series are a means for me to
reflect on the perfection and limitation of
our human experience."*

LEAH FAIRBANKS

right:

Moulin Rouge, 20 inches long overall. Leah Fairbanks and Debbie Nishihara. Lampworked soda-lime glass bead, with silver, gold, moonstone, pearls and pink tourmaline. *Photo: George Post.*

The creative jumble of Leah Fairbanks's studio is typical of the lampwork artist—especially those working with the colorful soda lime glasses often used in making beads. Nonetheless she creates soothing naturalistic renderings, well complemented in this piece by the metal work of Debbie Nishihara.

inset:

Moulin Rouge, (detail of back), 3 inches high. *Photo: George Post.*

Leah Fairbanks Working. *Photo: George Post.*

DOUGLAS M. FERGUSON

Inside Out Marbles, 1.5 inches diameter each. Lampworked borosilicate glass.
Photo: Melissa Ferguson.

The technique of "Inside Out" involves applying colored decoration to the surface of a tube, which is then manipulated to trap the color inside. Removing the air from within the tube draws the decoration down to achieve this dramatic, highly embossed effect. The fascinating optical effects of contemporary marbles are well illustrated in Ferguson's designs, which are among the most well respected in his field of specialty.

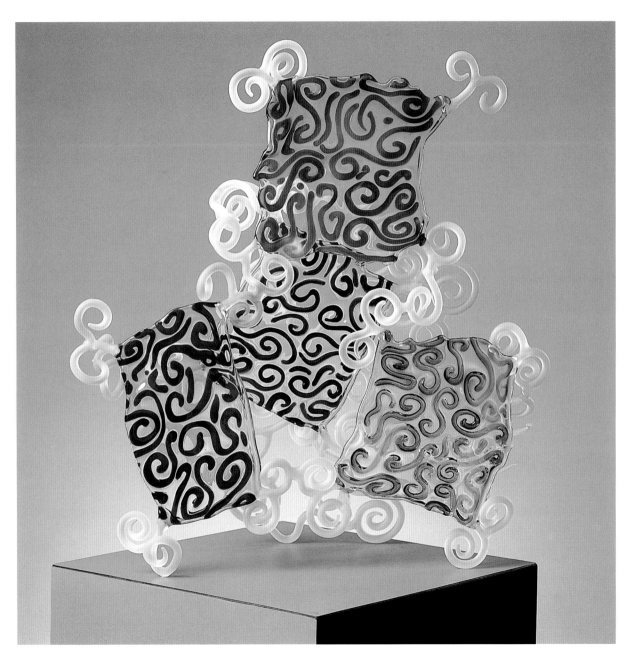

In Color Series, No. 92, Wavy-1, 20 inches high
19.5 inches wide 12 inches deep. Lampworked
borosilicate glass, sandblasted. *Photo: Charley
Akers.*

One of the first artisans to push the limits of scale
and respectability which had been attributed to
lampwork in this country, Hans-Godo Fräbel came
to the United States from Germany in the 1960s.
He set up a sophisticated studio for the production
of limited editions, and trained assistants to execute his designs with a high level of skill. Fräbel
Studios has ever since enjoyed an enviable repu-
tation as a source for elegant decorative work and
gifts of state for the U.S. government. Fräbel's more
recent personal work extends in a different direction, making dramatic use of color and pattern that
is in contrast to the more austere serenity of the
editions for which his studio is known.

SHANE FERO

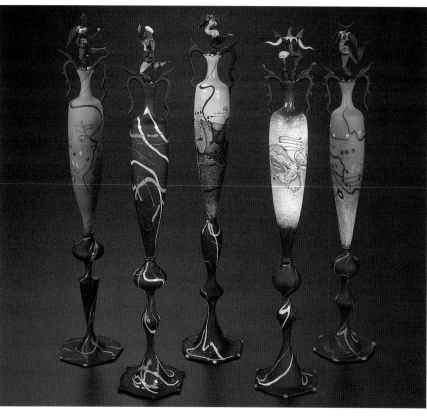

above:

Grouping of Spirit Vessels, 13.5 inches high, tallest. Flameworked soda-lime glass, acid etched. *Photo: John Littleton.*

right:

Tribute to Miró Series, 14 inches high 3.75 inches wide 3.75 inches deep. Flameworked soda-lime glass, acid-etched. *Photo: John Littleton.*

Shane Fero was an artist practicing lampwork technique long before it was fashionable or accepted to do so. He endured an apprentice's training in a traditional family of lampworkers, but quickly adapted the techniques he had learned to his own aims. As a student of philosophy, he developed a passion for creating objects in glass that would express the richness of the inner worlds he was exploring. Unattached to a particular material or way of working, his creations span the range from simple, delightful bottles to complex vessels and mixed-media figurative shadow boxes. As a respected teacher and lecturer, he continues to influence scores of lampworkers in this country.

Shane Fero's studio features several torches, including a classical cross-fire burner, traditionally used by neon sign benders.

A goblet begins with a "point"—a section of tubing stretched at the ends to form convenient handles.

Dots of colored glass are applied.

Heating and blowing shapes the bottom of the goblet bowl.

The lip is opened and flared in the crossfire burner.

Another section of tubing is decorated and stretched to form the stem.

At the bottom end of the stem, the foot is flared.

The two sections are fused together.

The finished goblet is checked for straightness.

SHANE FERO

GREG GALARDY

above:

Lizard Egg Series, 2.5 cm high overall.
Lampworked soda-lime glass, silver fuming.
Photo: Courtesy of the Artist.

Simple and elegant, Greg Galardy's beads
here illustrate the markedly distinct effects to
be had from basic variations on a decorative
theme. The degree of heat application, and
surface treatments such as acid etching, inter-
act with the unique properties of glass to yield
a very different but resonant result.

right:

Dew Drop Series, 1.5 cm high overall.
Lampworked soda lime glass, silver fuming.
Photo: Courtesy of the Artist.

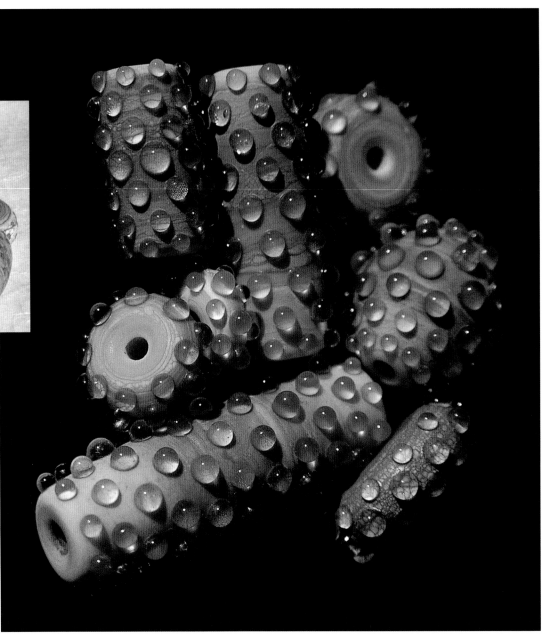

Sea Garden #1, 12 inches high, 24 inches wide 12 inches deep. Lighted Glass Sculptures. Borosilicate and uranium glasses; krypton, neon and xenon gasses; blacklight. Fabrication assistance by Thurston Levay, Jim Sato, Larry Albright, Tracy Martin. *Photo: Larry Lytle.*

"Light, energy and beauty are the subjects of my work. My sculptures are inspired by the fluid grace of the living beings that inhabit the translucent media of the sea where random order seems to rule in endless variation of form. With electricity I transform the noble gasses krypton, argon and neon, illuminating the forms to show the energy of life. Translucent and reflective, as the glass contains the light, the body and energy of the being come into view. Thus my invisible feelings for the natural world appear as jewels of light in glass."

KATHERINE GRAY

right:

Circles I Run In, 15 inches high 3.5 inches wide 3.5 inches deep. Musical bottle. Lampworked borosilicate glass. *Photo: Chris Brown Photography.*

"The bottle, when the music box is activated (playing "Close to You" by the Carpenters) turns slowly so that you can read the text through the bottle or through the surface of the oil. The text is 'Circles I run in.'"

far right:

Conjoined Cake Plate II, 22 inches high 15.5 inches wide 7.5 inches deep. Furnace blown and lampworked glass. *Photo: Roger Schreiber.*

Montage Beads, 3 inches high, tallest. Lampworked borosilicate glass. Montage technique. *Photo: Trevor Hart.*

The montage technique, which involves splicing colored sections of tubing into complex patterns, has been used here on an unusual scale. As a professional technical glassblower (and in fact, past President of the American Scientific Glassblowers Society), Doni Hatz has mastered the attention to detail and control of the material to execute these jewels from glass colored with oxides of silver, copper, germanium and cobalt.

KAZUYO HASHIMOTO

Woven Glass Dream 2, 60 cm high 43 cm wide 43 cm deep
Lampworked soda lime glass. *Photo: Courtesy of the Artist.*

Colorful yet refined, Hashimoto's "Woven Dreams" achieve
a visual depth and sensuality that draws us in yet gives us
pause with its evident fragility. In fact, the mutually reinforc-
ing strands of stretched glass give the works more strength
than meets the eye. Still, they convey a lightness and luminosity that is as ephemeral and precious as a dream.

KAZUYO HASHIMOTO

Woven Glass Dream 3, 90 cm high 27 cm wide 27 cm deep. Lampworked soda lime glass. *Photo: Courtesy of the Artist.*

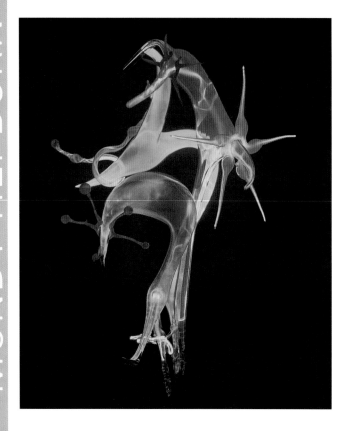

above:

A Fantasy in the Balance, 48 inches high 24 inches wide 18 inches deep. Static-charged luminous glass. *Photo: Courtesy of the Artist.*

right:

Garlic Flower, 84 inches high, 36 inches wide 36 inches deep. Static charged luminous glass. *Photo: Courtesy of the Artist.*

"Not visible in these photos is the motion of the arcs within the sculptures. Rare gas mixtures illuminated with static electricity create wonderful, undulating lines and snowflakes, similar in appearance to the Aurora Borealis. The use of static electricity enables the artist to illuminate any shape. The natural behavior of gas mixtures is a constant source of inspiration, as is the flowing motion of hot glass."

RYAN HIGGINS

above:
Grasshopper, 14 inches long 8 inches high 8 inches deep. Lampworked borosilicate glass. *Photo: Courtesy of the Artist.*

left:
Dragonfly, 19 inches high 19 inches wide 6 inches deep. Flameworked borosilicate glass. *Photo: Courtesy of the Artist.*

Clean stylizations of plants and animals, decorative innovations and the daring to tackle challenging technical problems are hallmarks of Ryan Higgins's work. His latest insects are quite large, and his skillful use of some of the technically difficult, newer borosilicate colors raises the bar for his colleagues while offering a tip of the hat to older traditions.

DINAH HULET

Jim's Wife, 16 inches high 14 inches wide 2 inches deep. Murrine assemblage; lampworked soda lime glass. *Photo: P. Hulet.*

"By creating the design (in my work, most often portraiture) inside the glass rather than placing it on the surface, as with painting or enameling on glass, the imagery takes on the fluid characteristics of the molten glass from which it is made. Through the use of this mosaic glass technique I am able to translate into visual form the imagery that fascinates me. And it is the imagery that is my focus—with technique as my tool."

Into My Life There Came a Man Called George, 12.5 inches high 17 inches wide 1.5 inches deep. Murrine assemblage; lampworked soda lime glass. *Photo: P. Hulet.*

YURI ISHIDA

Easter, 35 cm high 35 cm wide 35 cm deep.
Lampworked borosilicate glass. *Photo:
Courtesy of the Artist.*

The spiritual quality of clear glass is brought
to the fore in this sensitive vessel by Yuri
Ishida. We are reminded of the fragility of
peace, or of the delicacy of spring's new
growth.

TIM JERMAN

above:

Hermit Crab With Anemones, 9 inches high 5 inches wide 5 inches deep. Lampworked borosilicate glass. *Photo: Jerry Anthony.*

Tim Jerman's stylized creatures are fascinating decorative objects and a worthy twist on the centuries-old figurative tradition. Using real sea shells in some pieces, he creates simple yet intriguing renderings which invite closer inspection with their subtle wit and grace of line.

left:

Angler Fish, 4 inches high 5.5 wide 4 deep. Lampworked borosilicate glass. *Photo: Jerry Anthony.*

MARK JOY

above:
Why Plant Seeds? Where You Don't Want Them to Grow, 18 inches high 6 inches wide 3 inches deep. Neon and mixed media wall sculpture. *Photo: Courtesy of the Artist.*

right:
River Installation, 96 inches high. Neon light installation with water. *Photo: Courtesy of the Artist.*

The luminous gas of a neon tube is often used by artists to reference the life-force, the spirit energy which animates, inspires and sometimes confuses us. This seems to be Mark Joy's intention in these pieces which feel somehow both light and dark at the same time.

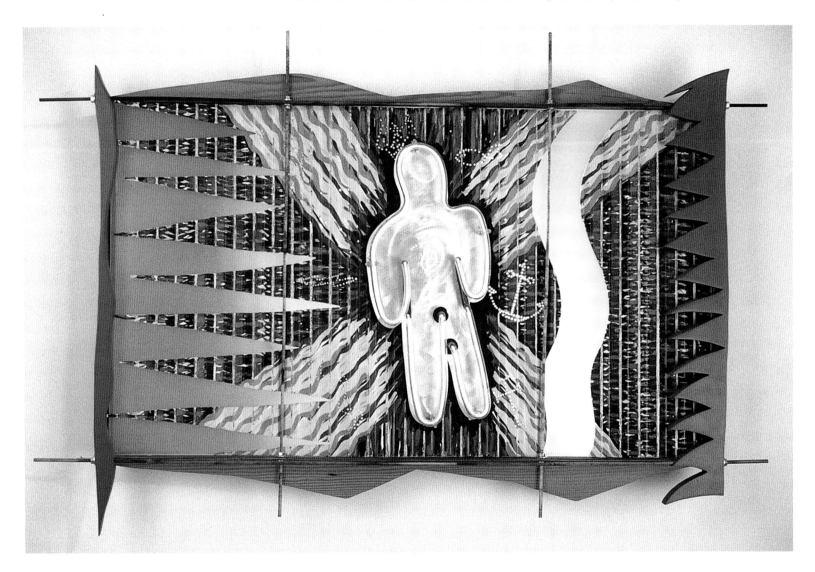

Existentialist Dilemma, 30 inches high 48 inches wide. Neon and multimedia. *Photo: Courtesy of the Artist.*

Who has not felt torn at some crossroads between fire and water, light and dark? Just as a luminous sign can command our attention on a busy street, the nimbus of light radiating from neon components in such an object as this confronts us and draws us into its glow. Neon can be both harsh and soothing as it bathes us in pure color, which quality Kehm has adeptly subsumed to his overall aim.

BRIAN KERKVLIET

right:

Lidded Knot Encalmo Chalice,

15 inches high. Lampworked borosilicate glass. *Photo: Courtesy of the Artist.*

An infectious spirit of fun pervades the work of Brian Kerkvliet. A pioneer in the resurgence not only of beadmaking but also of lampwork in general, he was a teacher of some of the artists in this book and hundreds of others less well known. His breadth of technical accomplishment includes not only lampwork, but flat glass techniques, fusing, offhand blowing, casting and almost anything else that can be done with glass. Always a learner himself, he continues to teach and spread the passion for lampwork at his idyllic farm studio in northern Washington State.

far right:

The Plateaus of Existence Give Light, 23 inches high 13 inches wide 3 inches deep. Lampworked and fused glass, lead and copper foil. *Photo: Courtesy of the Artist.*

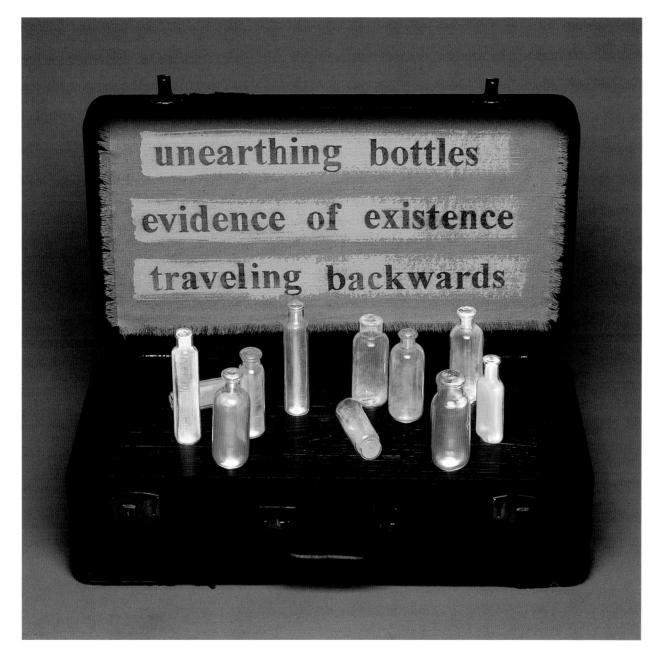

unearthing bottles

evidence of existence

traveling backwards

Furusato, 17 inches high 22 inches wide
14 inches deep. Neon and mixed media.
Photo: Larry Lytle.

Kim Koga has evoked the numinous, luminous quality of an archeaological discovery in this piece. Such historical and doc-
umentary concerns are also reflected in her
work as director of the Museum of Neon
Art in Los Angeles, which exhibits contemporary work in this fascinating medium.
This sculpture is like a small shrine to light
itself, and to the fascinations of discovery.

ERIKA KOHR

Before the Crossing, 10.75 inches high 6.5 inches wide 10.25 inches deep. Neon and mixed media. "Off hand" hot sculpted heart with single electrode. Sculpted heart and electrode have been joined hot through lampworking. *Photo: Paul Foster.*

"My work in glass art and mixed media strives to tell the story of the human condition. These 'narratives' are often autobiographical although they also tell the story of all women, all races and all people; finding common struggles from cradle to grave. This work also attempts to remind one of the human will to follow the path of greatest resistance with a willingness to face pain and adversity in the hope for a better life and a future that was not promised from birth. I strive to tell the story of immigration, of women, of the individual."

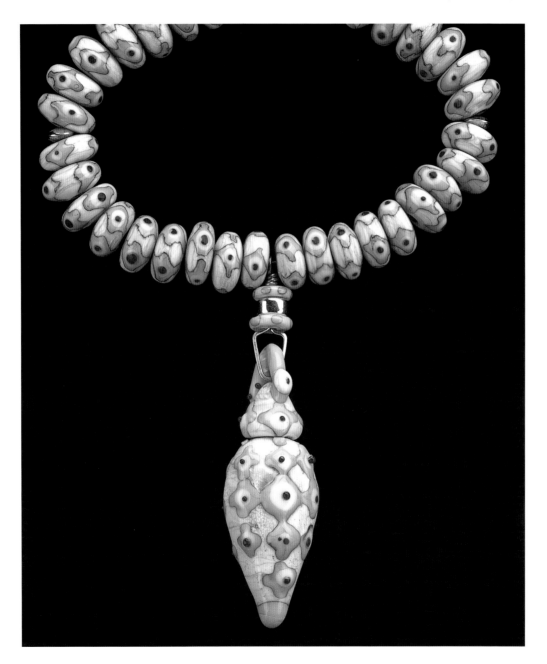

Prayerbead Necklace, 28 inches long overall. 108 bead mala (prayer bead) necklace with 14k gold accents and reclosable center bead. (detail view) *Photo: Paul Avis.*

Laura Lubin embodies a free but disciplined style which gives her beads and jewelry a reassuring, comfortable quality well suited to the prayer beads shown here. Her color sense, evident in all her work, also achieves a fine balance between simplicity and boldness.

KRISTINA LOGAN

above:

Brooch/Pendant, 2.75 inches diameter. Lampworked glass, sterling silver. *Photo: Paul Avis.*

right:

Green Teapot #4, 6.5 inches high 6.3 inches wide 3.75 inches deep. Lampworked and *pate de verre* glass. Mandrel-wound beads assembled to form handle and feet. *Photo: Paul Avis.*

"I am drawn to glass beads on a primal level. They are part of my lifelong fascination with art and ornamentation. Glass beads form an historical thread, connecting people and cultures throughout our history. Today we are still digging up beads that have been passed from hand to hand for centuries."

Kristina Logan begins one of her signature dotted beads by building up several layers of a base color. The basic technique of winding glass onto a wire mandrel using lampwork has changed very little in hundreds of years. Artists such as Logan have taken this simple method to new heights through painstaking experimentation.

With incense burning to enhance her meditative mood, Logan applies one dot after another with meticulous precision and relaxed concentration, beginning at the center of the bead.

Row after row of dots is applied.

A few last dots complete the composition.

ELIZABETH RYLAND MEARS

Accordion Book: 'The Naga Book,' 12 inches high 18 inches wide 6 inches
deep. Lampworked borosilicate glass, sandblasted, lustered, photographs.
Collaboration with daughter, L. Lindsey Mears. *Photo: Tommy Olaf Elder.*

Standing Book: 'The Bone Woman,' 12 inches high 10 inches wide 8 inches deep. Lampworked borosilicate glass, sandblasted, lustered, photographs. Collaboration with daughter, L. Lindsey Mears. *Photo: Tommy Olaf Elder.*

"On Collaborations With My Daughter: When my daughter was just a little girl, she occasionally spoke words that stopped me short. My head shook in absolute recognition. Could this life journey have such a soulmate? Was it the all knowing wisdom emanating from that small person that created such wonderment? A greater bond grew at the root. We were Babas at each end of the selfsame thread. Our brains and souls were joined by that woven link. Messages rippled to and fro. As she grew, she withdrew from that connection, as she must, to experience the world and find her own voice. She is now a mature young woman, with all the wisdom she possessed as a child. The thread of understanding has been renewed."

ELIZABETH RYLAND MEARS

RICHARD MEITNER

Schrödinger's Cat, 91 cm high. Lampworked borosilicate cat, offhand blown base and sphere, colored water (in sphere), iron coating. Lampwork fabrication by Edwin Dieperink, base by Oberglas. *Photo: Ron Zijlstra.*

An American artist working in Amsterdam, Richard Meitner conceives visual statements which are cerebral while remaining organic. He is true to the essential properties of glass, but not limited by the material. Working in tandem with craftsmen who execute the components of his compositions, he often references science—or our ideas about science—with a wry wit and a knack for visual punning.

left:

Dorado, 29 inches high 11 inches wide 5 inches deep. Lampworked borosilicate glass; graal technique, sandblasted. *Photo: Dan Abbott.*

Robert Mickelsen plays classical geometric themes of composition against organic forms and surface patterns. The result is dramatic and architectonic, and he continues to explore larger and larger scale for his pieces, using high-tech machinery for some aspects of their production. A major figure in lampworked art, he teaches workshops and writes about the field for several national publications.

far left:

Borealis, 27 inches high 17 inches wide 6 inches deep. Lampworked borosilicate glass; graal technique, sandblasted. *Photo: Dan Abbott.*

ROBERT A. MICKELSEN

JANIS MILTENBERGER

this page:

First Attempt, 37 inches high 13 inches wide 13 inches deep.
Lampworked borosilicate glass, sandblasted, oil painted.
Photo: Lynn Thompson.

*"You have to think a piece through and give a lot of consideration to
the construction—when you put what together. Sometimes—on the
stick houses in particular—I tried to think, 'how would a bird build
this?' I made and constructed it stick by stick. Basically, I enjoy the
material, it's become my friend: very dependable, consistent. I feel I
know what it will do and won't so well within the context of what I
make. Mostly I think about life, people, society, compassion and how
I can address these things in my work."*

facing page:

Given For You, 20 inches high 26 inches wide 16 inches
deep. Lampworked borosilicate glass, sandblasted, oil painted.
Photo: Lynn Thompson.

WILLIAM MORRIS

Artifact Grouping, 14 inches high, tallest. Blown glass, steel stand. *Photo: Rob Vinnedge.*

The sculptural animals and artifacts of William Morris are brought into being through a combination of "offhand" and lampworking techniques. The expressive details of form evidenced here can only be achieved using a hand-held torch at the gaffer's bench. The scale and sheer volume of heat available at the furnace merges with the advantages of lampwork, enabling the artist to create work that is unique and compelling.

WILLIAM MORRIS

Panther Comb, 10 inches high 11 inches wide 3 inches deep .Offhand blown and torch worked glass, steel stand. *Photo: Rob Vinnedge.*

JAMES MINSON

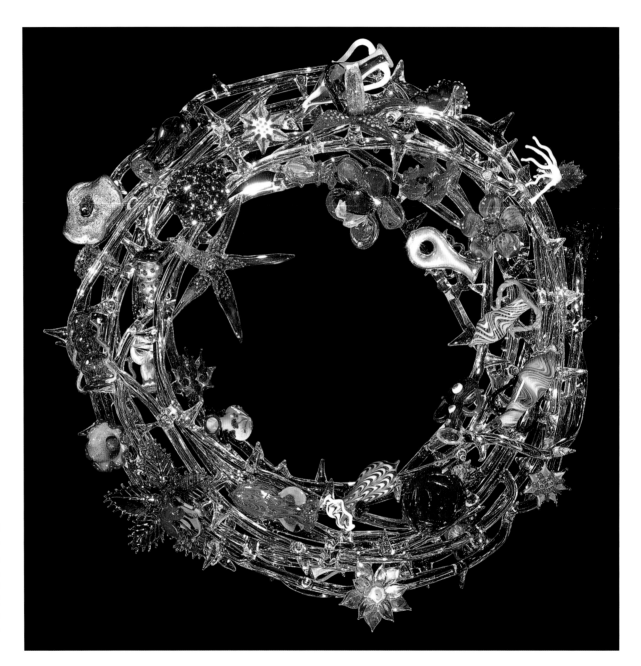

Wreath, 18 inches diameter 8 inches deep. Lampworked borosilicate glass. *Photo: Spike Mafford.*

James Minson, in his Wreath sculptures, takes the additive quality of lampwork to the ultimate extreme. Building layers of decorative, structural and symbolic forms into a unified, flowing whole, he has created a motif which could be read as a swirling vortex of mental imagery—with a clear, still center inviting contemplation of life's complexity from a peaceful perspective.

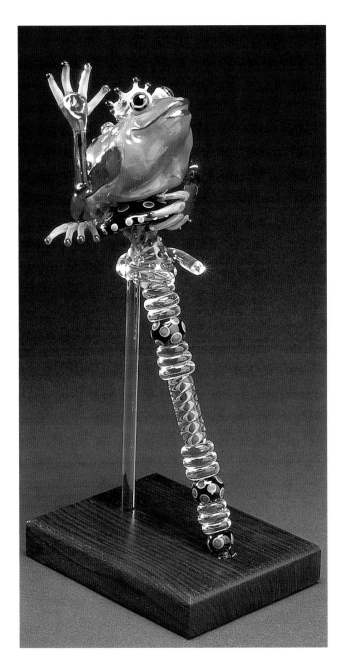

above:

By the Light of the Moon, 8 inches high 12 inches wide 12 inches deep Lampworked and cast glass. *Photo: David Harrison.*

left:

Frog Queen, 11 inches high. Lampworked borosilicate glass rattle. In the stem is a section of cane with an internal ribbon twist. *Photo: David Harrison.*

Nancy Nagel's whimsical blown animal caricatures are born of meticulous technique. Unabashedly bright and cheerful, they welcome the viewer into a playful fantasy world of childlike wonder. Her unusual use of the rattle form reinforces both the playful and magical qualities of her designs, which are sculpted from clear tubing coated with colored rods or powder.

DON NIBLACK

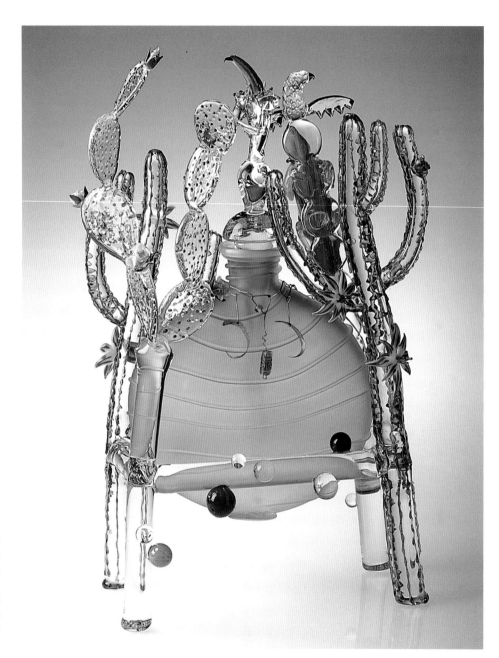

.Stilted Bottle: 'Sonoran Desert,'
22 inches high 12 inches wide 5 inches deep.
Stopper design inspired by Shane Fero.
Lampworked and furnace blown glass.
Photo: Courtesy of the Artist.

Combining lampwork technique with offhand
blown glass, Don Niblack has created an
assemblage that is both personal and out-
going. The central bottle is blown at the furnace, while the stilted armature is formed at
the lamp. Like some other artists, Niblack finds
this a satisfying way to bring the diverse properties of glass together into one object.

KEVIN O'GRADY

left:
Luxor, 3 inches high 2.5 inches wide 1 inch deep. Lampworked borosilicate glass cuff bracelet. *Photo: Jeff Scovil.*

above center:
Tsunami, 3 inches high 2.5 inches wide 1 inch deep Lampworked borosilicate glass cuff bracelet. *Photo: Jeff Scovil.*

Kevin O'Grady has brought a new dignity to single-piece glass jewelry. His sophisticated use of color and the optical properties of borosilicate give his bracelets an elegance that has not always been associated with glass adornments. His marbles are the result of long experimentation to enhance the effects achieved through an unconventional use of tubing. His application of color begins at the back surface of his objects, and is built up in successive layers like a reverse painting. Condensing the glass to thicken it intensifies the magnification that can be achieved.

above right:
Sea Floral, 1.5 inches diameter. Lampworked borosilicate marble. *Photo: Jeff Scovil.*

above:

Inner Carnival II, 9 inches high 9 inches wide 3 inches deep. Lampworked soda lime glass, enameled and copper electroplated plate glass. *Photo: Courtesy of the Artist.*

A small pantheon of archetypes occupies the psychic carnival depicted in this surreal mixed media composition. The piece can be seen as an odd twist on the tradition of figurines that might occupy one's shelf as novelties or light amusements. Pat Owens's skill at the torch is evident in her expressive renderings as shown in the detail image, while her sense of the figure and of the individual "characters" portrayed is both engaging and disquieting, reflecting the inner voyage implied in the title.

right:

Inner Carnival II, (Detail) *Photo: Courtesy of the Artist.*

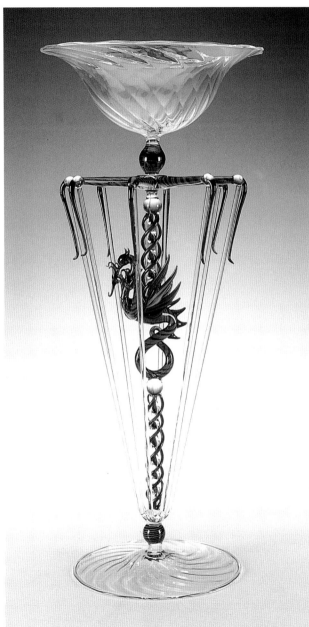

DOUG REMSCHNEIDER

far left:
Dragon's Lair, 20 inches high 8 inches wide 8 inches deep. Decorative bottle; lampworked borosilicate glass. *Photo: Jonathan Wallen.*

Doug Remschneider's elaborate goblets and sculptures evoke a classical, Old World mood through distinctly contemporary means. Built up in the additive manner, which is lampwork's hallmark, they achieve, in the end, a stable but light and balanced composition.

left:
Caged Dragon Goblet, 12 inches high 5 inches wide 5 inches deep. Lampworked borosilicate glass. *Photo: Jonathan Wallen.*

ROGER PARRAMORE

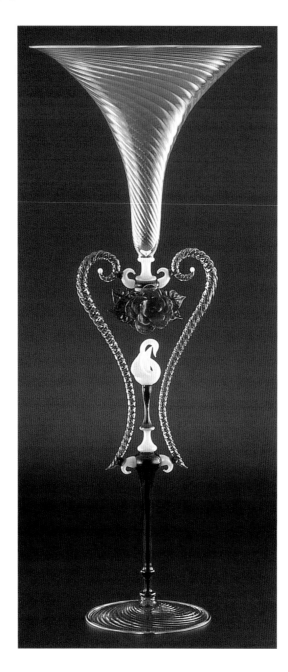

right:

Swan Cup, 24 inches high.
Lampworked borosilicate glass.
Photo: Courtesy of the Artist.

far right:

Cups, 22 inches high, tallest.
Lampworked borosilicate glass.
Photo: Courtesy of the Artist.

*"I'm particularly interested in the con-
tinuity of lines. So for me, working
with really thick glass is tantamount
to working with a really fat Magic
Marker." What I do with the glass is
try to work the surfaces (the inside
surface and the outside surface) as
close to one surface as possible....
The closer you can get, in essence, to
having the two surfaces become one,
the closer you are to actually working
with pure line."*

Roger begins forming the bowl of his goblet by connecting a section of tubing to a punty of solid glass. This demonstration was given at the Penland School of Crafts.

Heating, blowing and stretching begin to define the shape.

The shape becomes more defined.

The lip is opened by stretching the heated glass until it is thin enough to vaporize in the flame.

Using heat, gravity and centrifugal force, Roger flares the lip of the bowl.

A smaller section of tubing is shaped and flared in a similar way.

Special ribbed tubing is used to form an optic section for the stem.

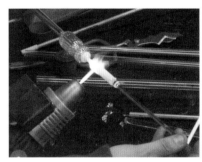

Colored rod is added for the stem.

Colored glass is added to the other side.

More glass is added and stretched.

The foot is sealed onto the stem and flame-annealed.

The bowl is similarly fused onto the top end of the stem.

ROGER PARRAMORE

91

MARC PETROVIC

Float, 13 inches high 13 inches wide 8 inches deep. Furnace blown and hot worked glass. *Photo: Cathy Carver.*

Marc Petrovic combines masterful use of a portable torch with traditional offhand glass-blowing techniques to create his sculptures. Time (elapsed or suspended), the natural world, and its intersection with the things of men are persistent themes in his body of work.

His execution of a raven at the 2001 Glass Art Society conference in Corning, New York is also illustrated here.

The raven begins as a bubble from the glass-blower's furnace.

Specialized pincers are used to start defining the shape of the bird.

After reheating with a torch, Petrovic uses shears to separate the feathers on wings and tail.

The wings are stretched and laid into position against the body. Then a tungsten pick, heated with a torch, is used to "drill" a small vent hole under one wing. This is necessary because the head will soon be separated from the blowpipe and sealed. Without a vent, the hollow body would expand and deform when heat is applied.

After connecting the base of the raven to a punty rod, and removing the original blow-pipe, Petrovic uses a brass tube to inflate the head through the vent hole.

A bit is brought to form part of the beak.

After adding more glass and finishing the beak, the location of the left eye is heated with a torch.

A quick press with a brass tube shapes the eye. Detail is added with a dental pick.

The mouth is reheated with a torch, and a commemorative murrine is inserted.

The finishing touches are given to the beak. (The full sequence of photos excerpted here can be seen in *Contemporary Lampworking*, by Bandhu Dunham.)

MARC PETROVIC

SALLY PRASCH

above:
Buddha Flower, (Detail) *Photo: Tommy Olaf Elder.*

right:
Buddha Flower, 14 inches high 6 inches wide 6 inches deep. Flameworked borosilicate glass. *Photo: Tommy Olaf Elder.*

In addition to her career as an artist, Sally Prasch is an accomplished fabricator of chemical apparatus. The execution of her creative pieces bears the mark of her technical virtuosity, enabling her to pursue ideas and design concepts unattainable without mastery of the medium. In the classes she teaches at craft schools and studios around the world, she leads students through unconventional explorations of the material (toasting marshmallows on a glass spit, fabricating an orchestra of glass instruments and the like) which open new creative horizons for the next generation of glass artists.

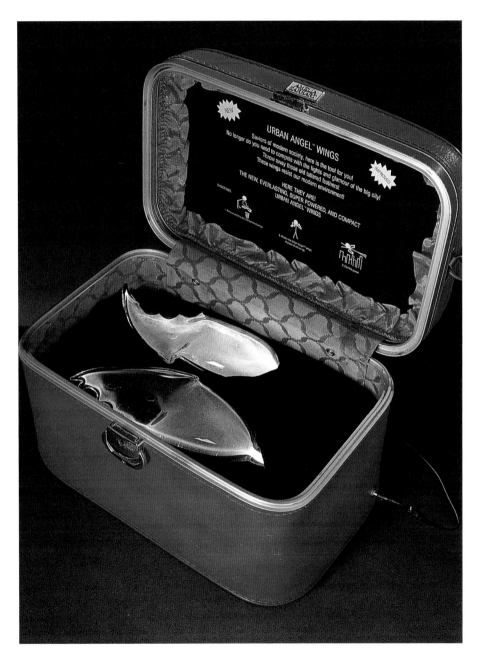

Urban Angel, 9 inches high 14.5 inches wide 9 inches deep. Offhand blown and torch manipulated glass, mixed media. *Photo: John Horner.*

Like some of the other neon and plasma works in this book, this work was created for one of the annual "Traveling Light" exhibitions held in conjunction with the Glass Art Society conference. Artists were challenged to design luminous sculpture that would fit in and make use of a conventional piece of luggage. Asya Reznikov has blown these clever angel's wings "offhand" at the furnace and manipulated the shape using lampwork techniques. Powdered phosphor coating inside the blown forms enhances the luminosity of the gas, injected at a low pressure. This piece uses electrodeless technology, meaning that the enclosed gas is stimulated to glow by radio waves from a small transmitter in the base of the sculpture.

RENÉ ROBERTS

Stonework Collection, 2 inches long, largest. Lampworked soda lime glass with copper, silver, iron and gold colorants. *Photo: Hap Sakwa.*

The combination of precious metals with glass produces remarkable and often unpredictable results. René Roberts skillfully exploits this potential in the luscious surface of her mandrel-wound and core-formed beads. Simple shapes are complemented by the complex, subtle, and sometimes dramatic patterns resulting from the chemical interactions of metal and glass in the variable atmosphere of a torch flame. Art and alchemy are brought together in small, potent units of creative expression.

René Roberts demonstrates applying silver leaf to a core-formed bead.

Burnishing the leaf with a graphite paddle to help it adhere to the surface. Additional application of heat gives mottled and iridescent effects.

GINNY RUFFNER

above:

Frilly Modernism, 15 inches high 28 inches wide 18 inches deep. Lampworked borosilicate glass, mixed media. *Photo: Mike Seidl.*

left:

Smelling Surprise Flower Basket, 10 inches high 22 inches wide 15 inches deep. Lampworked borosilicate glass, sandblasted, mixed media. *Photo: Mike Seidl.*

America's first lady of flamework, Ginny Ruffner broke the boundaries of accepted practice in the 1980s to bring lampwork technique fully into the Studio Glass movement. Challenging artistic prejudices with humor, energy and the charm of a southern belle, she combined lampworked glass with other media—including her original discipline of oil painting—to create surprising and engaging objects which quickly won her great respect. In her teaching work she has influenced scores of artists, including quite a few represented in this volume. A past President of the Glass Art Society, she continues to produce lampworked and mixed-media sculpture of a remarkable range from her studio in Seattle.

right:

Banded Vessel Series, 19 inches high 9 inches wide 9 inches deep. Furnace blown and lampworked soda lime glass, chemically bonded. *Photo: Cathy Carver.*

far right:

Phoebe Robin's House, 19 inches high 8 inches wide 8 inches deep. Furnace blown and lampworked soda lime glass. *Photo: Cathy Carver.*

In the collaborations of this husband-wife team, Kari works at the torch creating intricate organic lattices from canes pulled by hand at the glassblower's furnace, while Marc fabricates the blown ware, birds and fruit "offhand." In both cases, delicate variations in color come from powdered glass or frit in which the glass is rolled before shaping. The use of powder for color application makes very naturalistic effects possible and, in the case of the straight canes, lends a unique translucency to the material, enhancing the tender quality. The house forms, regarded by the team as primarily Kari's work, often embody themes of domestic life or the delicacy of our organic existence, as reflected in her reference to "Phoebe Robin's House" as a "house of cards."

Marc Petrovic also does completely independent work, which can be seen on page 92.

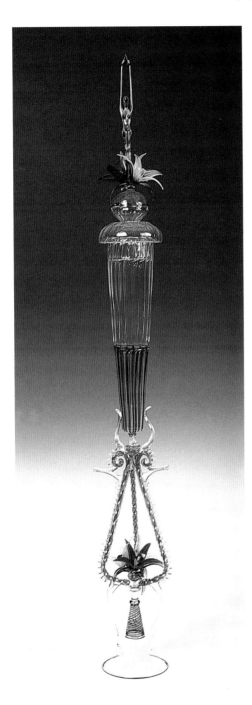

EMILIO SANTINI

left:

Donna Floreale, 28 inches high 5 inches wide 5 inches deep. Lampworked borosilicate glass. *Photo: Rick Nelson.*

Born and raised in Venice, Emilio Santini comes from a traditional family of glass-blowers. Now residing in Virginia, he continues to express his ancient roots—in his own inimitable style—in objects of consummate skill and sophistication. Moving freely between the challenges of different glass formulas (soda lime or borosilicate) he shares his passion for the material not only through his prolific body of work, but also his generosity as an instructor in studio workshops all around the US.

far left:

Primavera, 24 inches high 5 inches wide 5 inches deep. Lampworked borosilicate glass. *Photo: Rick Nelson.*

TORU SATO

above:

Lidded Container, 7.5 cm high 7.8 cm wide 7.8 cm deep. Core-formed lead glass. *Photo: Endo.*

The technique of core-forming originated in ancient Egypt before the invention of the blowpipe in Syria during the first century BC. This method of making vessels happens to be quite popular in Japan. The Satake glass produced in that country, with its low viscosity and melting point, is very well suited to this work. Toru Sato is one of Japan's foremost practitioners of core-forming, which involves wrapping thin rods of glass around a refractory core to define the interior surface of the vessel. The delicate floral elements are prepared ahead of time and applied after the initial layer is completed. His method requires a refined sense of heat control as well as patience, persistence and long periods of concentration.

right:

Glass with Floral Motif, 8.6 cm high 4.6 cm wide 4.6 cm deep. Core-formed lead glass. *Photo: MGM.*

EMIKO SAWAMOTO

inset:
Tropical Flower Arrangement, (Detail).
Photo: Rich Images

left:
Tropical Flower Arrangement, 12 cm high.
Photo: Rich Images.

These sweetly rendered plant forms reflect an attention to minute details and a love for the simple beauty of nature. Reminiscent of *ike-bana*, Sawamoto's charming flower arrange-ments—like her jewelry and beads—reflect a high level of compositional and technical skill.

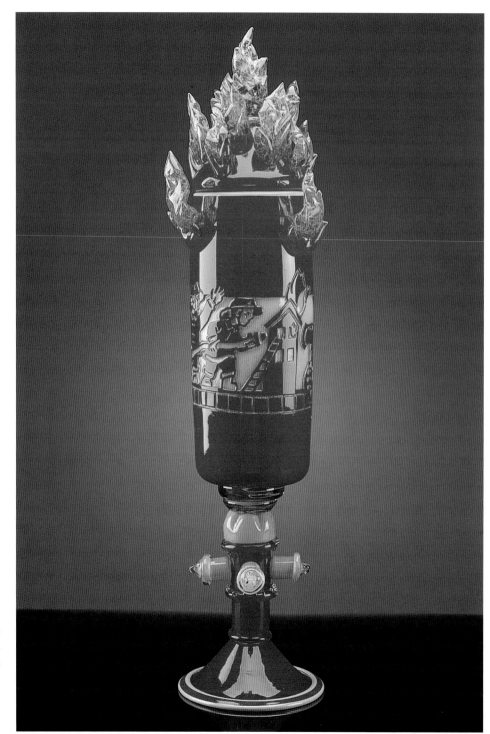

The Firefighters II, 29 inches high 7 inches wide 7 inches deep. Combination offhand and lampworking technique, sandblasted. *Photo: Bill Lemke.*

Working at the gaffer's bench, the artists add components and details to their lidded goblets using lampwork techniques. Sandcarving the central image completes the narrative.

ALISON SHEAFOR

above:

Abacus Goblet: Artifact, 11 inches high 4 inches wide 4 inches deep. Flameworked borosilicate glass, with glass beads. *Photo: Nathan Ham.*

left:

Abacus Goblet: Ladder, 12 inches high 7 inches wide 5 inches deep. Flameworked borosilicate glass, with glass beads. *Photo: Nathan Ham.*

These witty and seemingly impractical goblets contrast the fluidity of the material with the strict integer system of the abacus on formal and conceptual levels. The abacus is rigid and "digital," yet kinetic with its loose glass beads. The core of the goblet form is firm and functional, yet fluid and dynamic in design. These are glasses to make you think while you drink, or at least keep count of how many you've had!

BARBARA BECKER SIMON

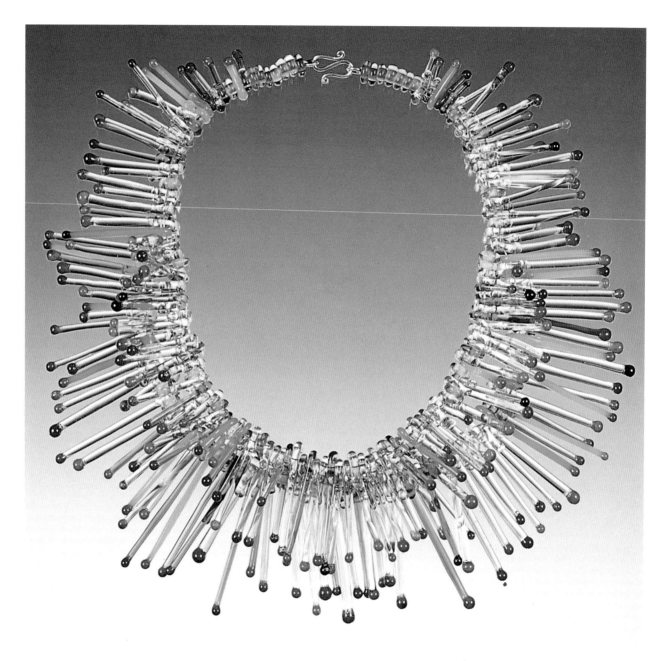

Cool Stix Necklace, 9 inches high 9 inches wide .5 inches deep. Lampworked soda lime glass, enamels. *Photo: Rob Stegmann.*

"This necklace was inspired by sea anemones, cacti, and the stiff neck ruffs of Elizabethan clothing. When it is worn, it does not lay flat, but spikes up, dynamically, in many directions, catching the light. Since each element is created and strung individually, I was able to use every type of glass available to me (borosilicate, Effetre/Moretti, Satake, and Czech glass) in order to realize the color palette that I had in mind—no worries about incompatibility. Application of enamels to the ends of the "stix" adds a punch of color."

PAUL J. STANKARD

far left:

Botanical Column with Masks, Flowers, Figures & Insects, 7.25 inches high 4.25 inches wide 4.25 inches deep. Flameworked, kiln-cast, cold worked and laminated glass. (Front view) *Photo: James Amos.*

A respected elder of the contemporary lampwork renaissance, Paul Stankard began his training as a scientific glassblower, graduating from the unique program at Salem Community College, where he now teaches in addition to pursuing his creative work. His paperweights and larger botanical forms are renowned and collected around the world. Combining lampwork and casting techniques, he creates plant forms with "organic credibility," complementing them with elements of organic litter, encased text, subtly rendered figures or most recently, masks which bring a new mystical element into his compositions.

left:

Botanical Column with Masks, Flowers, Figures & Insects, 7.25 inches high 4.25 inches wide 4.25 inches deep. Flameworked, kiln-cast, cold worked and laminated glass. (Back view) *Photo: James Amos.*

LOREN STUMP

above:

Kabuki, (Detail). *Photo: Rich Images.*

right:

Kabuki, 11.5 inches high 5 inches wide 5 inches deep. Lampworked soda lime glass, kiln assembled. *Photo: Rich Images.*

Loren Stump achieves the unprecedented level of decorative detail in his larger figurative pieces by a kiln assembly technique he developed through extensive experimentation. A specially constructed kiln enables him to reach in and assemble components in a perfectly controlled atmosphere, without which such compositions would be impossible. Stump is a master of murrine fabrication, and these pieces enable him to make full use of his abilities with mosaic canes.

A Long Voyage Home, 24 inches high 48 inches wide 10 inches deep. Lampworked glass, neon, mixed media. *Photo: Larry Lytle.*

At the age of 15 David Svenson began working at a nonprofit center in Alaska that supported the training of Native American wood-carvers in the old traditions, which were in danger of dying out. Since then he has continued to develop relationships with local woodcarvers and has even been adopted into a clan of the Tlingit people. His respect for the renewal of Native culture he has witnessed inspired this piece, in which light returns to the image of an abandoned village.

JEFFREY A. SPENCER

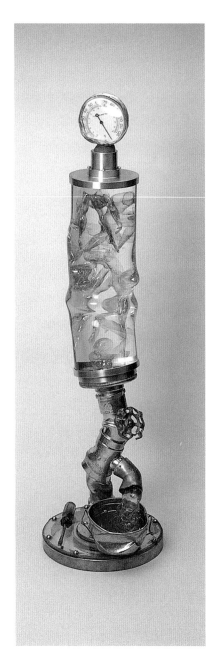

left:

Meltdown, 32 inches high 9 inches wide 9 inches deep. Flameworked glass, mixed media. *Photo: Courtesy of the Artist.*

Jeffrey Spencer's adept use of mixed media complements his sensitive relationship to the human figure. As a former Olympic athlete and a practicing Chiropractor, he has intimately studied the human body and its capacity for gesture. Themes of entrapment and liberation, struggle and triumph run throughout his work.

far left:

Second Chance, 44 inches high 17 inches wide 21 inches deep. Flameworked borosilicate glass, steel. *Photo: Courtesy of the Artist.*

above:

Oversize Necklace, (detail). Lampworked glass, anodized aluminum. *Photo: Danielle Thompson.*

left:

Pulley Necklace, 21 cm diameter. Lampworked glass and 925 silver. *Photo: Isamu Sawa.*

"I find technology, the history of technology and people's attitude to technology an inspiration. Technology as an extension of the human hand—tools, machines and mechanics—informs the processes I use, the materials I choose and the forms and elements I build into my jewelry.

"As society moves quickly towards a world increasingly dominated by digital technology, I like to refer to how things work and how things used to work. My necklaces are formed with precisely made repeated components, convey the feel of a factory, of industry and machines."

CÉSARE TOFFOLO

above:

Colonna, 30 cm high. Lampworked and cast glass. *Photo: Studio Norbert Heyl, Murano.*

A native of Murano, the Venetian island of glassblowers, Césare Toffolo's skill is unsurpassed. His elegant compositions are frequently complemented by tiny human figures in naturalistic poses which seem to give them a greater level of detail than the eye can see. In addition to his creative work at the torch, Toffolo is the founder of Centro Studio Vetro, an educational institution which publishes a journal and offers classes in traditional Venetian glass techniques, in a bold break with ancient traditions of secrecy on the island.

right:

Natura Morta, 50 cm high. Lampworked glass, mixed media.
Photo: Studio Norbert Heyl, Murano.

Hoshanos, 12 inches high 23 inches wide 15 inches deep. Lampworked soda lime glass. *Photo: Courtesy of the Artist.*

A master not only of lampwork but also off-hand glassblowing, Gianni Toso was born in Venice but now lives in Baltimore. His extraordinarily detailed figures often, as here, reflect the love for his Jewish heritage, as well as the figurative traditions of his native land. The engaging detail of his figural groups and chess sets has made them highly sought-after by collectors.

VICTOR TRABUCCO

Blueberry Inclusion, 12 inches high.
Lampworked and coldworked glass
Photo: Courtesy of the Artist.

Victor Trabucco's paperweights reflect his meticulous attention to detail as well as superb skill. An engineer by training, known to consult with the Steuben factory on difficult technical issues, he is unlimited in tools and ingenuity with which to pursue his love of glass. His large encasement sculptures have surpassed the definition of "paperweight" and make sophisticated use of the reflective and refractive properties of extremely pure optical crystal.

Swallowtail, 4 inches diameter. Lampworked glass, cold worked. *Photo: Courtesy of the Artist.*

MILON TOWNSEND

Green Moray, 5 inches high 5 inches wide 5 inches deep. Lampworked borosilicate glass. Assisted by Ryan Higgins. *Photo: Tommy Olaf Elder.*

Milon Townsend achieves visual depth in his paperweights through the skillful use of powdered glass and frit, as well as graceful, gestural compositions of the plants and animals that inhabit these small worlds. An author and teacher known for pushing the limits of preconceptions about lampwork, he has influenced scores of artists through classes, books and videos.

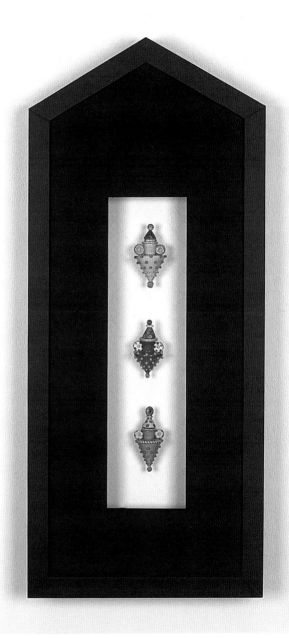

above:

Vessel Trio, 3.5 inches high each. Lampworked hollow-formed glass. *Photo: Melinda Holden.*

left:

Amphora Abode, 28 inches high 13 inches wide. Lampworked hollow-formed glass. *Photo: Melinda Holden.*

Heather Trimlett's tiny blown vessels, originally conceived to be worn like a pendant, are precious and domestic, yet with an architectural quality that is complemented effectively in the house-like frame of the "Amphora Abode." In the absence of a tubular form of her preferred glass, the technique in making these objects is truly a miniaturized version of offhand glass-blowing, in which she gathers softened soda lime glass on the end of a tiny blowpipe, shaping it in a gas-oxygen flame.

TOSHIKI UCHIDA

above:

Fossil, 2.0 cm diameter. Lampworked lead glass; mandrel-wound. *Photo: Courtesy of the Artist.*

Toshiki Uchida's beads are unique and rich in surface detail. He often works below the surface as well, encasing naturalistic patterns in veils of clear or translucent color. At one moment shimmering like a droplet of water, and the next, rough and softly pitted like a gently worn river pebble, Uchida's individual beads are delightful details in a rich visual world.

riight:

Flora, 2.2 cm diameter. Lampworked lead glass; mandrel-wound. *Photo: Courtesy of the Artist.*

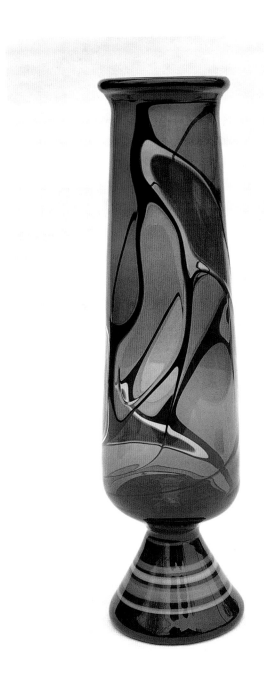

KURT WALLSTAB

left:

Vase, 31 cm high 6 cm diameter.
Lampworked soda lime glass; montage technique. *Photo: Courtesy of the Artist.*

far left:

Vase, 21 cm high 5.6 cm diameter.
Lampworked soda lime glass; montage technique. *Photo: Courtesy of the Artist.*

Kurt Wallstab of Griesheim, Germany, is one of the consummate masters of the montage technique, which involves splicing individual sections of colored tubing in complex patterns. The use of soda lime glass, which has the best working properties and color for this technique, but which is prone to cracking throughout the process, adds another level of challenge to this already difficult approach. The results of this struggle are well worth it, however, as born out by the pieces shown here.

117

WARNER WHITFIELD

above:

Rainbow Perfume Bottle Collection, 6 inches high 3 inches diameter. Lampworked borosilicate glass. *Photo: Jonathan Wallen.*

The clean and appealing wares of Warner Whitfield are a high point of lampwork studio production. Although available in multiples, each piece is masterfully executed with individual attention.

right:

Northern Lights Ornament Collection, 9 inches high overall. Lampworked borosilicate glass. *Photo: Jonathan Wallen.*

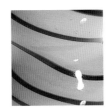

GLOSSARY OF
LAMPWORKING TERMINOLOGY

For more information on the lampworking techniques and processes described here, see *Contemporary Lampworking: A Practical Guide to Shaping Glass in the Flame,* also by Bandhu Dunham.

ANNEALING: Raising the temperature of a piece of glass in order to relieve internal strass. The glass becomes imperceptibly soft, allowing stresses to relieve themselves through fluid motion without losing the shape of the glass. The appropriate annealing temperature for a borosilicate glass like Corning 7740 (Pyrex™) is 560 °C (1040 °F). The annealing process consists of four steps: heating the glass to annealing temperature; soaking at annealing temperature; cooling slowly to 75°C below annealing temperature; cooling more quickly to room temperature. Some artists also add a soak at the strain point.

ATMOSPHERE: In lampworking this refers specifically to the conditions within the torch flame. The atmosphere of the flame can be "oxidizing" (high in oxygen) or "reducing" (low in oxygen). A reducing atmosphere will affect some colored glasses, especially lead-based glasses, turning the surface black or otherwise changing the color. A flame that is reducing is generally softer and cooler than a flame that is oxidizing. Glass color is also sometimes affected by the atmosphere within the kiln during annealing.

AVENTURINE: Glass with particles of undissolved copper distributed throughout. It has a sparkling, gold-like appearance, similar to the mineral for which it is named. The effect is achieved by super-saturating a batch of glass (in the furnace) with copper until the metal crystallizes out.

AVOLIO: A spool-shaped bit of glass used to join goblet stems to bowls and feet.

BEAD RELEASE: A compound applied to a mandrel to facilitate the removal of a finished bead. *The Bead Release* is also the name of the newsletter of the International Society of Glass Beadmakers.

BIT: A small amount of glass used either as decoration (a bump) on the surface of a piece, or as "glue" connecting components together.

BLEB: The small bump of solid glass on the end of a tube. This is formed when the tube has been sealed by pulling glass from the end.

BLOWHOSE: A rubber hose connected to a piece of glass tubing so that the tubing can be blown and shaped without being placed in one's mouth. Blowhoses are often fitted with a swivel so the tube can be rotated without tangling the hose.

BOROSILICATE: Any silicate glass having at least 5% Boric Oxide (B_2O_3). Developed originally for railroad lantern lenses and fabricating scientific apparatus, this class of glasses is commonly used for artistic lampworking as well. Corning Pyrex™, Schott Duran™, Kimble Kimax™ and Northstar Borocolour™ are common borosilicate glasses.

BUTT SEAL: To connect two rods or tubes end-to-end, making one long piece.

CANE: Glass rod, often with colored decoration.

CENTIGRADE: A temperature scale in which the freezing point of water is 0° and the boiling point of water is 100°. Sometimes also called "Celsius," after the scale's inventor, Anders Celsius. Centigrade temperature is equal to five-ninths times thirty two degrees less than Fahrenheit temperature.

COMB: A decorative technique of dragging a tool across the surface of molten glass to distort an applied design. See also "Feathering."

STEPHANIE SERSICH
Party Necklace, 18 inches long overall. Lampworked soda lime glass, sterling silver. Individual beads decorated with bits of clear and colored glass. *Photo: Robert Diamante.*

COMPATIBILITY: Two glasses of the same or closely matched thermal coefficient of expansion (COE) are said to be compatible because they are stable when combined. This means that they expand and contract at the same rate as their temperature change, effectively behaving as one material. Glasses which are not compatible will crack or burst apart when the joint between them cools. Compatible glasses are also said to "fit."

CORDS: Visible striations in a piece of glass, caused by variations of the chemical composition (such as the introduction of air or dust, or the uneven mixing of component chemicals).

CORE-FORMING: The technique of forming a glass vessel by coating a destructible core with glass. When the glass is cool, the core is removed, leaving a hollow vessel. This technique was used by the Egyptians before the invention of the blowpipe to make hollow vessels.

CRIMPS: Another name for "mashers"—the tool used to flatten glass, sometimes impressing it with a pattern. The tool consists of two metal plates attached to a tweezer-like or plier-like handle. In Italian, *borsellissie* describes plain flat crimps, while *borsella puntata* is a set of crimps with texture on them.

DEVITRIFICATION: Crystallization of glass. Glass which is heated incompletely or unevenly during working can turn foggy looking and dull on the surface because the glass has begun to crystallize. Chemical impurities on the surface of the glass can also cause devitrification.

DICHROIC GLASS: Glass which has a thin metal coating applied to the surface, giving it a reflective tint. The glass will appear one color in reflected light (light bouncing off the glass) and another in transmitted light (shining through the glass), therefore the name: di- (two) chroic- (from chroma, color).

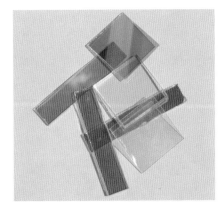

DICHROISM: The exhibition of one color in reflected light and another in transmitted light (such as in gold fuming, where the glass looks like metallic gold in reflected light, but pink, violet or blue when light shines through from in back). Also refers to glasses which appear different colors under different lighting conditions.

DIDYMIUM: A shorthand name for a combination of the two rare earth elements, neodymium and praseodymium. This mixture is included in the glass used to make filter lenses for lampworkers. The filter lenses absorb much of the dangerous infrared and ultraviolet radiation from hot glass, as well some of the yellow flare-off created by hot glass in the flame.

FAHRENHEIT: A temperature scale devised by Gabriel Daniel Fahrenheit, in which 32°F is the freezing point of water, and 212°F is the boiling point of water. Fahrenheit temperature is equal to thirty-two degrees more than nine-fifths times the Centigrade temperature.

FEATHERING: A specific type of decorative combing in which a tool is dragged on the surface of a hot piece of glass at right angles to a series of parallel lines.

FENICIO: The Italian name for festooning, or complex patterns of combed lines.

FILIGRANA: Glass rod (cane) consisting of a colored center surrounded by clear glass.

FIRE-POLISHING: Smoothing the surface of a sharp or rough piece of glass by careful heating in the flame. As the glass softens, surface tension will draw it into a smooth contour.

FIT: Sometimes thrown by frustrated novice glassblowers. See also "Compatibility," above.

FLAME ANNEALING: The process of annealing glass in a torch flame, instead of in a kiln. It is carried out by gently heating the glass to a temperature just below its softening point, and then allowing the entire object to "soak" at that temperature for a few minutes before gradually reducing the temperature of the glass. The glass is cooled slowly by moving it gradually out of and away from the flame.

FLARING: Spreading out the end of a tube or an open bubble to create a wider opening—such as the mouth of a vase or the lip of a goblet.

FLAMEWORKING: Another term for lampworking. Some people are passionate about which term should be used; they are used interchangeably in this book.

FRIT: Crushed glass. Finely ground frit is called powder.

FUMING: A vapor deposition process in which a thin film of metal (usually silver or gold) condenses on the surface of a hot piece of glass. Depending on the thickness of application, fuming results in either a color tint, an iridescent color or a shiny metallic surface.

JENI & DEL WOOCK
People Champagne, 10 inches high. Lampworked borosilicate and soda lime glass. Goblet with flared bowl and foot. *Photo: Hap Sakwa.*

FUSED QUARTZ: Glass formulated from pure silica (SiO_2), which is highly resistant to chemical attack and thermal shock. Commonly used in extreme high-temperature applications for research work.

GAFFER: In offhand glassblowing, the master glassblower or head of a team ("shop") of glassblowers. The gaffer sits at the glassblowing bench and does most of the manipulation of the glass, directing assistants to prepare components or help in other ways.

GOB: A quantity of soft glass.

GRAPHITE: A crystalline form of carbon, commonly used in glassworking tools because it does not burn or stick to glass. The same material pencil "lead" is made from.

HARD GLASS: A common name for borosilicate glasses and others that melt at high temperatures, as opposed to "soft" glasses such as lead and soda-lime. There is no absolute definition of "hard" and "soft" in this usage; they are relative terms.

HEAT: A measure of the total amount of kinetic energy in the atoms which make up an object. This is not the same as "temperature." It takes more heat to boil a quart of water than a teaspoonful, even though the change in temperature is the same.

HEAT BASE: The amount of heat in a piece of glass. To "read" the heat base is to assess not only the amount of heat in the glass, but also to note its distribution throughout the object. This "reading" provides the basis for estimating how much more heat to apply to the glass when working it.

HOBNAIL: A regular pattern of closely spaced, raised dots.

IKEBANA: The japanese art of flower arranging.

IRIDIZING: A decorative technique involving spraying hot glass with metallic salts (such as stannous chloride, $SnCl_2$) to give an iridescent finish.

KILNWASH: A watery mixture of kaolin clay and alumina hydrate which prevents glass from sticking to metal or ceramic surfaces when hot. Used to coat molds so that the glass can be removed more easily and also to coat mandrels as a bead release.

LEADED GLASS: This term refers to pieces of flat glass which are held together by lead either in the form of extruded strips called "came" or as solder in the copper foil technique. Traditional stained glass windows are examples of leaded glass. Glass formulations which are fluxed with Lead Oxide (such as "Lead Crystal") are not properly referred to as "leaded glass." They are "lead glass."

LINEAR COEFFICIENT OF EXPANSION (LCE): See "Thermal Coefficient of Expansion."

DEBBIE CROWLEY
Blue Banded Butterfly Fish, 2.25 inches high 2.88 inches wide. Lampworked soda lime glass. Mandrel-wound bead. (The hole left from the mandrel passes from the underside where the display rod enters, through the top of the body.)
Photo: Courtesy of the Artist.

MANDREL: The rod or wire on which a glass bead is wound (wrapped). Stainless steel welding rod is the most commonly used type of mandrel, but other possibilities include brass rod, rolled copper foil, bamboo splints and ceramic rods.

MARIA: An expanded area in a rod or tube, formed by compressing the length of the glass.

MARVER: As a noun, this refers to a flat table-like surface on which glass is shaped. As a verb, this refers to shaping glass by rolling it on any nonflammable flat surface. Marvering also chills the surface of the glass, making it a helpful tool in adjusting the heat base of an object.

MELTING POINT: Defined by ASTM as the temperature at which a round fiber of the glass in question, .65 millimeter in diameter and 235 millimeters long, will elongate under its own weight at a rate of one millimeter per minute when the upper 100 millimeters of its length is heated at the rate of 5 ±1 °C per minute. Basically, this is the temperature below which the glass acts as a solid and above which it can be shaped. Viscosity at the melting point is about 103 poise.

MERESE: A disk-shaped blob of glass in the stem of a goblet. Often mereses are located at the junction between the stem and the bowl or foot.

MILLEFIORE: Derived from the Italian for "a thousand flowers," this term refers to symmetrical patterns made from slices of radially symmetrical, flower-like mosaic cane designs. "Millefiore canes" are the rods from which these slices are made. Patterned canes themselves, whether flower-like or not, are really "mosaic canes." Millefiore is a special case of the mosaic cane. Slices of cane that are not flower-like are best referred to by the more generic term "murrine" (singular, "murrina"). The common use of the diminutive "millie" to refer to any type of murrine is unfortunate, but perhaps unstoppable by now.

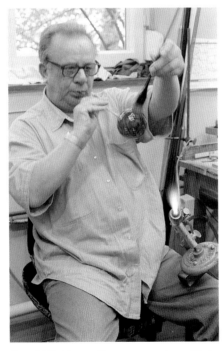

MONTAGE: An assemblage of several pieces of tubing, usually of different colors, that is then blown out into a final form. Often the montage is twisted or otherwise altered to give

Kurt Wallstab, working on a montage. *Photo: Courtesy of the Artist.*

complex patterns of color. Montage is a variation of encalmo technique. The consensus seems to be that if there are more than three sections joined together, an encalmo becomes a montage.

MOSAIC CANE: A special glass rod formed from a variety of colors. The colors are assembled in one of several ways to produce a gob of hot glass, the cross-section of which is a colored pattern. The gob is then stretched into a rod (cane) and sliced into thin wafers. Each wafer (called a murrina) bears a miniature version of the original pattern.

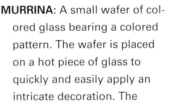

Assorted mosaic canes by Brian Kerkvliet. *Photo: courtesy of the artist..*

MURRINA: A small wafer of colored glass bearing a colored pattern. The wafer is placed on a hot piece of glass to quickly and easily apply an intricate decoration. The plural is murrine. When embedded in a glass object, the colored insert is called a murrino. See also Millefiore and "Mosaic Cane."

NEON: An element, one of the "noble gasses," used for illuminated signs and luminous sculpture. When excited by an electrical current in a closed envelope, neon will glow red. Other gasses give different colors of light, but the term "neon" often refers to any signs or artwork using illuminated gasses. See also "Plasma."

OFFHAND: The technique of shaping glass at the furnace, using metal blowpipes and rods dipped into a tank of molten glass. Also referred to as "Furnace" or "Free Hand" glassblowing, or simply "Hot Glass."

OXIDIZING: High in oxygen. An oxidizing flame is typically hotter and more sharply defined than a reducing flame.

PLASMA: Ionized gas. Luminous sculptures that use a single electrode (or radio waves, without any electrodes) to stimulate gasses with static electricity are refered to as "Plasma sculpture."

POINT: A section of glass tubing with drawn handles (tapers) at either end. This is a convenient way to handle and work with large diameter tubing. Also used to refer to variations in COE when discussing compatibility. A difference of 1×10^{-7} is called one point. Glasses whose COE differ by more than two or three points should not be combined.

GREGORY A. KRAMER
Three Nobles of Naz, 17 inches high, tallest. Cast and fabricated steel, glass, neon, argon xenon. *Photo: Courtesy of the Artist.*

POISE: The unit of viscosity. One poise is one Newton-second per square meter, or one gram per square centimeter per second.

PRUNT: A decorative and functional blob of glass on the outside surface of blown ware.

PUNTY: A temporary handle attached to a glass object to facilitate working. A punty joint is intended to be less structurally sound than a standard fusion between two pieces of glass. The punty can be snapped off cleanly when the piece is finished. From the French, *pontil*.

REDUCING: Low in oxygen. A reducing flame may draw oxygen out of hot glass, discoloring the glass surface. Lead glass, for example, will turn black because lead oxide at the surface is being reduced to metallic lead. Adding more oxygen to the flame, and heating the glass out in the end of the flame if necessary, will eliminate reduction. Some color formulas are designed to make use of reduction effects intentionally.

ROD FORMING: Shaping glass by covering a metal rod, such as in core-forming and making mandrel-wound beads.

RONDELLE: A round disk of glass formed by spinning and flattening an opened bubble.

SEED: A tiny bubble in a piece of glass.

SILICON: Silicon is an element, represented by the atomic symbol, Si. It is commonly found in the form of Silicon Dioxide (SiO_2), also called Silica. Silica is a major component of all common glasses. Silicone (with an "e") is a type of rubber, commonly used as an adhesive and sealant.

SLUMPING: Sagging, generally to make glass conform to a mold in a kiln.

SOAK: To hold a piece of glass at a given temperature for a specified period of time. For example, glass that is being annealed must be soaked at the annealing temperature to allow the stresses within the glass to be released.

SODA: Properly speaking, Sodium Oxide (Na_2O). But in general use among glassblowers, "Soda" refers to Sodium Carbonate (Na_2CO_3).

SOFT GLASS: This refers to a type of glass—a chemical formulation—not a technique. It is also a relative, and not very precise term. Glass formulas that have a relatively lower melting point and a longer working range are referred to as being "softer" than a glass that is stiff at the same temperature. The term comes from the way the glass feels when working it. Perhaps coincidentally, glasses that are softer when hot are usually softer (on the Mohs Hardness Scale) when cold also. Generally, when people refer to "soft glass" they mean a soda-lime or lead glass, such as Effetre Moretti, Kugler, or Satake—as opposed to "hard" borosilicate glass.

STRAIN: Physical deformation of a material under stress, defined mathematically as the deformation divided by the original length of the object.

STRAIN POINT: The temperature at which glass undergoes an internal configurational shift somewhat analogous to freezing. Below this temperature, any stress created in the glass will dissipate when temperature equilibrium is reached. The annealing cycle must be designed to cool the glass very slowly to a temperature well below the strain point.

STRESS: A force exerted on a material. In the case of glass, we are typically interested in stresses within an object, such as those caused by uneven heating above the strain point. Stress is also caused by external forces, such as hanging a weight from a glass object or bending it. Stress takes the form of either compression or tension. Stresses created in a glass object while it is manipulated in the flame can cause it to crack later. It is the sum total of stresses within an object that cause it to crack. Stress is measured as force per unit area. See also "Annealing."

STRIKING: Heating a colored glass above its normal annealing temperature (but below softening temperature) in order to bring out its true or full color.

SUPPIALUME: Italian for "lampworking."

THERMAL COEFFICIENT OF EXPANSION: (aka COE, LCE, α) The relative amount by which a material will expand (per degree) when heated. Expressed as an exponent, i.e., for Pyrex™ 7740, COE = 32.5 X 10-7. This is about one-third the COE of most soft glasses. The smaller the COE, the more resistant the glass is to thermal shock. Two glasses which have largely different COE's should not be joined directly together.

THERMAL SHOCK: The strain created by abruptly heating or chilling a piece of glass.

TRAIL: A thin line of colored glass, typically wound around a glass object in a spiral.

TWISTIE: A decorative glass cane made of two or more colors twisted together. Lines of colored glass can be also applied to the surface of a clear rod, or trapped within layers of clear, the latter forming an internal ribbon twist.

VERMICULITE: Expanded mica. Used as an insulating material to prevent glass from cooling too quickly, as a prelude to annealing.

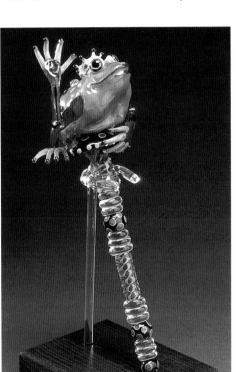

NANCY NAGEL
Frog Queen, 11 inches high. Lampworked borosilicate glass rattle. In the stem is a section of cane with an internal ribbon twist. *Photo: David Harrison.*

VISCOSITY: Viscosity is a scientific measurement of a fluid's resistance to flow. Technically, it is the fluid's internal friction, which is caused by molecular attraction. The "thicker" a fluid is, the more viscous it is said to be; the more drippy and runny it is, the less viscous. Honey is more viscous than water. Viscosity is measured in units called "poise."

VISCOSITY GRADIENT: A gradation in the fluidity of a piece of glass. For example, it is easiest to control a sphere of hot glass on the end of a rod when the glass is softest at the far end of the sphere, and progressively more stiff (viscous) in the direction of the rod. This is a viscosity gradient. The gradient can be undermined by unwanted hot spots or cold spots in the glass, which makes the glass harder to control.

VÒLTA: (Muranese) The best process or system of making a glass object.

WORKING RANGE: The temperature range in which glass is workably soft.

INDEX OF ARTISTS

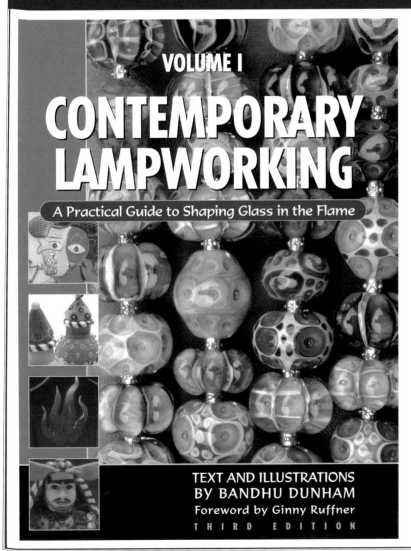